# DATE DUE

# AMERICA REVISITED

The Earl of Birkenhead, P.C.

# AMERICA REVISITED

BY
### THE EARL OF BIRKENHEAD, P. C.
(FREDERICK EDWIN SMITH)

*Essay Index Reprint Series*

## BOOKS FOR LIBRARIES PRESS, INC.
### FREEPORT, NEW YORK

First Published 1924
Reprinted 1968

LIBRARY OF CONGRESS CATALOG CARD NUMBER:

68-16911

TO MR. JUSTICE DUFF
OF THE SUPREME COURT OF THE DOMINION OF CANADA
AND TO MR. PAUL D. KRAVATH
OF THE BAR OF NEW YORK
AND HONORARY BENCHER OF GRAY'S INN
THIS BOOK IS DEDICATED
IN MUCH FRIENDSHIP
BUT WITHOUT COMMITTING EITHER OF THEM TO ANY OF
THE OPINIONS HEREIN EXPRESSED

# PREFACE

NEARLY six years ago the duty was imposed upon me, at a critical period of the War, of travelling the United States for the purposes of War propaganda. I had not on this occasion the opportunity of visiting the extreme West or the extreme South. But otherwise I was given the opportunity of addressing great audiences of American citizens in almost all the principal centres of population. The experience was naturally one of extreme interest; but the circumstances were too exceptional to afford a safe basis for any generalisation upon Anglo-American relations. For one thing, the atmosphere was too charged with electricity, and even with emotionalism. For consider what had happened.

President Wilson had quite evidently formed the opinion almost from the outbreak of war that his was to be the high function of the conciliator. Most clearly he was of the opinion that no occasion would or ought to arise in which the United States would be engaged as a belligerent. And accordingly he delivered from time to time stately orations in which he absolutely refused to treat any moral distinction between any of the belligerents. An intelligent student of the world crisis must, if confined for purposes of information to the speeches of President Wilson and to those speeches alone, have reached the conclusion that the nations of Europe, reacting to the stimulus of insane ambitions, had plunged into a bloody war; and that on the whole, in relation to merits, there was very little to choose between them. The published works of the principal German diplomat at Washington had made it abundantly plain how great was the influence he had established over the mind of President Wilson; how frequent and how friendly were the discussions; and

how easy it would have been for him to pre-
serve indefinitely an intimate diplomatic relationship if he could have been protected
from the maladroit naval megalomania of
the German admiralty. President Wilson,
indeed, evidently believing that war-weari-
ness would in the last resort drive the nations of the world to accept his arbitration,
and detecting in this exalted rôle no contingent rival but His Holiness the Pope, had
made up his mind to hold the scales evenly
between the two schools of belligerents.
And in this easy determination he pictured
himself at some time in the future in the
capacity known to the classical authorities
of Roman Law as *vir pietate gravis,* dictat-
ing to an admiring world the terms upon
which the controversy, which in his view
should never have arisen, might be happily
composed. No one who had occasion, as I
had, closely to study the diplomatic correspondence which took place at the critical
period between the United States of Amer-

ica and this country, could doubt that this was the self-conscious object of the policy of the ex-President. He did, it is quite true, address remonstrances to the German Empire, growing with the passage of time continuous and stronger, upon the submarine campaign. But he was always careful to supply judicial equipoise by sending to St. James's very verbose protests upon the subject of the freedom of the seas. And an extremely attentive observation of all the diplomatic correspondence for which President Wilson was responsible makes it impossible to contend that until the moment when by a precarious majority he was re-elected President, he had deflected his bias in the slightest degree more upon the one side than upon the other in this controversy. In other words, until the period which I have adopted as crucial, he had not afforded the slightest indication that he regarded the morality of one side of the combatants as in any way distinguishable from the morality of that of the other. And indeed, the issue upon which he deliberately allowed his lieutenants to present his presidential campaign showed how indeterminate even at that date were his conclusions upon matters which were surely not lacking in the materials for a definite judgment. The slogan of the campaign in the critical electioneering States was prescribed by authority: "He kept us out of the War."

And then, quite suddenly, there came a culmination of outrage, insult and contempt issuing from Berlin which no great, proud and powerful nation could support. The battery, in other words, before which France had recoiled in impotent protest for twenty years was directed upon Washington. Outrages were officially planned to destroy American factories which were doing exactly what German factories had done in the Russo-Japanese War. Innocent merchantmen flying the American flag and plainly identified in other ways as Ameri-

can vessels were sunk by German sub-
marines. Finally a clumsy German diplomatic intrigue was disclosed which had as
its purpose to enlist disturbed Mexico by
the side of Germany to meet the contingency
of a rupture with the United States. This
culmination of events finally disturbed the
equipoise of President Wilson.

In a noble, even if slightly belated phrase,
he cried, "The challenge is to all mankind.
The wrongs against which we now array
ourselves cut to the very root of human
life."

The observation is not perhaps unreasonable that this conclusion, so vividly expressed, was the same which had driven a
pacific British Cabinet in August, 1914, to
precisely the same conclusion. So pacific
indeed was that Cabinet that their Ministers
resigned because they were not prepared to
undertake any responsibility for the war.
And it might even be added that the data
necessary to the conclusion reached by Eng-

land had not been very obviously multiplied between the two periods.

But critical examination as to the mental attitude of the American Government in the intervening period and as to the decisive character of the various agencies of enlightenment which changed that attitude do not very specially belong to this place, although they may hereafter be made the subject of useful examination.

It is, however, very relevant to my present purpose to recall the enthusiasm with which this great and resourceful people flung themselves into the task of war, when once they were permitted to do so by their leaders. And I had the good fortune to visit the country soon after the signal had been given from the White House to let loose the dogs of war. An unforgettable impression was produced upon my mind by the superb and massive effort which I saw everywhere in progress before my eyes. We left a Europe the political morale of which had almost everywhere been impaired, whose finances were shattered, and whose man power was gradually failing before the bloody demands of the far-flung trenches. We came to a puissant and populous empire, intact in strength, immensely reinforced, by neutral trade, in material wealth, and zealous to contribute a white heat of moral enthusiasm which was the more formidable because it had been pent up so long. It was in such an atmosphere that I was privileged on the invitation of the American Government, and as a Minister of the British Government, to make the acquaintance at this critical and deeply interesting time of hundreds of thousands of American citizens. Never shall I forget the enthusiasm of those days; never the affectionate and devoted friendship of those many Americans who were flinging everything into the common cause. It is indeed unlikely that in our lifetimes, or perhaps in the lifetimes of our children, any occasion will happen so apt to bring together

American and British hearts. British officers were everywhere assisting to train American battalions: American ships of war were co-operating with British ships at Queenstown, now under the command of a British Admiral, now under the command of an American Admiral. And suddenly Washington completely forgot about the freedom of the seas: for I can state with considerable personal knowledge (I was Attorney-general at the time and responsible for the Crown cases in Prize) that the activities of the two Fleets upon the relevant matters were not very obviously distinguishable from the earlier activities of the British Fleet.

It is indeed an unprofitable and a slightly ignoble question, Who won the War? For all who co-operated in that glorious victory were perhaps necessary for its attainment. But no competent witness can deny the supreme contribution which the American nation made, even at a late period, when the

energies, the man power, and the material
resources of the veteran combatants were
flagging and declining. For this at least was
certain of the American people, that however slow they might be in entering upon a
quarrel, when once involved therein, they
were capable of exhibiting a doggedness and
a tenacity second to that of no people in
history. And though I have read, I think,
almost all the great books which have appeared on the subject of the War, I do not
think that full justice has ever been done
to the effect produced by the American intervention upon the morale of our enemies.
The German nation, though docile, disciplined, and in some respects even servile,
was nevertheless both educated and intelligent. And naturally an Army which was
the Nation (if one eliminates the old men)
reflected both the intelligence and the educa-
tion. The Army knew perfectly well that
if there were half a million American troops
in Europe in January, there would be a mil-

lion and a half in June, three millions next
January, and perhaps in a year six millions.
And they knew too that behind those millions, vigilant and resolute, were arrayed the
material wealth and the industrial genius of
the wealthiest and one of the most virile nations of the world. And so it happened just
at that moment of all others, when the fortunes of the German Armies required the
equal maintenance of military and civilian
morale, that the morale of both was dissipated and destroyed. For the civilians and
the soldiers alike realised that the quarrel
had become hopeless; and that the longer it
was prolonged, the more prodigious would
the ultimate humiliation prove.

The submarine gamble was the greatest
which any nation has ever undertaken in the
throes of a desperate war. It was undertaken in the belief that it would produce
decisive results before the United States
could make themselves effectively felt in the
War.

# PREFACE

The calculation failed.

The arrogance of the German Admiralty was corrected by British doggedness; and America so effectively and so swiftly entered into the War that the courage and stamina of the great German Empire withered before her victorious incursion.

It would have been unreasonable on a visit paid at a moment of unavoidable war reaction and disillusionment to hope that one might recapture all the spirit of the old days. There exists in America to-day a great and general apprehension that the country may still be entangled in European politics. And this apprehension is strengthened by the unfavourable view which most Americans have adopted of the present tendency of those politics. In the first place they are naturally not well informed as to the *nuances* of the latest European developments. They see around them little evidence of European resettlement; everywhere they hear of wars and rumours of wars; they see no promise of a fresh dawn; and in the gloom which precedes the dawn, they congratulate themselves once more that they rejected the rosy and glowing visions of President Wilson.

But this attitude, which I believe to be true of the nation taken as a whole—though it is rash to generalise upon what a nation so far-flung and so cosmopolitan as America is thinking—is consistent with a very sincere spirit of friendship to this country. The extent of that friendship must not be exaggerated. The United States have been reinforced from many fountains of emigration which draw little from the England of Elizabeth and Shakespeare. For the first time last year in the New York Directory the patronym of Cohen displaced the Smiths from an age-long supremacy. To many millions in the United States it is still hardly a recommendation to a visitor that he should be an Englishman. These facts should all be noted in cool perspective. And yet it should equally be remembered how warm-hearted, how generous and how sentimental in the best sense the American people is. And it must equally be remembered that millions of the most enlightened citizens in this great Republic consistently exhibited in the face of every difficulty a warm and generous friendship for Great Britain, never ceasing in the critical days of the War to affirm their clear view of the moral responsibility of the United States; and that they have ever since rendered a generous measure of recognition to the superb effort which Great Britain by general admission made in the War.

And so, as I pass by way of Preface to some of the speeches delivered in the United States or in Canada which I here reprint, many grateful memories throng my mind of old and new American friends, of kindly and warm-hearted hospitality. Nor do I, though not by temperament oversanguine, exclude the hope that year by year and decade by decade these two great peoples, re-

# PREFACE

sembling each other so closely in their general outlook upon the major problems of civilisation and humanity, will still re-create in its fullness the generous friendship which was the happy fruit of an unhappy War.

All the speeches reprinted in this volume were delivered either in the United States or in the Dominion of Canada except my Rectorial Address before the University of Glasgow. I include it in the volume because it correlates and somewhat expands the point of view which pervades the American speeches. It was stupidly and ignorantly assailed principally by persons who had studied it in headlines. Strangely enough it was never criticised upon its weakest side; namely, that it added little to the volume of ascertained and established truth.

BIRKENHEAD.

# CONTENTS

xxiii

# AMERICA REVISITED

## CHAPTER I

### THE UNITED STATES TO-DAY

(1) *Material Prosperity.*

Each time that I visit the United States I am conscious of an enormous advance in the material prosperity of this illimitable country. But I confess that on the present occasion the impression was deeper than ever before. Everywhere I went I saw cities developing with incredible rapidity. Everywhere factories are being extended. Everywhere great public buildings conceived upon a scale of nobler architecture are coming into existence. And the United States are evolving a special quality of

architecture which does not any the less owe
something to the American type that it is
founded in its essential features upon Greek
conceptions. I am not here speaking, of
course, of the skyscrapers of New York.
These are indeed among the wonders of the
world. And those who conceived them are
entitled to take a high place among the
architects of the world. For they devised
something altogether original, extremely
difficult, and at the same time quite indispensable if the majestic and variegated life
of New York was to continue on a site so
narrow and so congested. And they have
dealt with a problem which no other nation
has had occasion to approach with a scheme
of inventiveness which, however bizarre,
possesses a character and a genius of its
own. No one who upon a summer evening
has approached these towering edifices,
overtopping the lower clouds in their tall
beauty, can fail to realise an almost magic
city, peopled indeed by the eager searchers

2

after wealth and surrounded for some space
by main streets, but nevertheless a splendid
emblem of the aspiring greatness of this immense republic.

The architecture of the larger cities is
matched by the public spirit and munificence of the wealthy citizens of this country. One great university after another is
enriched by the munificence of private bene-
factions. The University of Chicago is
modelled architecturally with mimetic fidel-
ity upon the noblest buildings of Oxford and
Cambridge. Here is to be found an almost
exact replica of the great Hall of Christ-
church, unfavourably distinguished only by
the portraits which are ranged upon its
walls. Nor is it alone in the great centres
of wealth like Chicago that an admirable
sense of civic responsibility operating upon
immense wealth has produced illustrious
universities. In the States it is almost universally realised that the accumulation of
wealth upon a large scale involves and

renders natural a bestowal of some portion of it upon generous public purposes.

In Great Britain we are still able to note with admiration many evidences of the same spirit. But the creation within so short a period of time of so many provincial universities had unquestionably congealed the fountain of private munificence in relation to our greatest universities, Oxford and Cambridge. Here the rich stream of mediæval endowment has failed, and the two most illustrious universities in the world have been forced, not without great peril to their essential character, to look to public resources.

Twenty-five years ago the average American man of business was conceived of, and not altogether with injustice, as one who left home early and returned late, employing the long day in the feverish interests of Wall Street; he became dyspeptic at forty; and he very often died at fifty. In the interval (if he were successful) he accumulated a vast fortune. His wife and his beautiful daughters enjoyed it, and so far as he was concerned, the rare alleviations of a hectic life coincided with a few hurried visits to Europe.

I never was quite able to realise what such a man derived from life commensurate with the exertions that he made. The Psalmist after all said that the life of man was three-score years and ten. Persons gifted with exceptional constitutions have very readily and agreeably to themselves prolonged this period. There is, for instance, still living in the United States of America an old lady aged one hundred and twenty-six; and she gave a tea party on the occasion of her last birthday. At such an age it might very reasonably be assumed that a tea party on such an anniversary is a very enjoyable occasion. But not to reason from an extreme case, the late Lord Halsbury learned to ride a bicycle at the age of eighty, and to play golf at the age of eighty-two. I do not know whether he rode the bicycle well or badly, though the evidence is overwhelming that he played golf very badly; but in any event he undoubtedly enjoyed both. I myself have never been able to understand the philosophy of life of the men who, unless they dislike life, overdraw their accounts at the only vital bank that really matters. After all, however much wealth one has, it is as certain as anything can be that at the last dreadful moment it must be left behind. Charon's fare may be as readily paid by the pauper as by the prince; indeed there is every reason for believing that in the last resort you may be ferried over that stream without any contribution at all.

I think there is a great change in this respect in the outlook upon life entertained by most successful business men since I first visited America nearly thirty years ago. And oddly enough, the modest instrument which in my judgment has done most to pro-

mote this change has been the game of golf.
When I first knew America I should doubt
(though I do not know) whether there were
more than twelve golf links in the whole of
the United States. The late Mr. Gladstone
was once, much against his wishes, compelled to play golf. He is reported to have
commented upon the experiment that it was
a good walk spoiled. Such would undoubtedly have been the verdict thirty years ago
of any ninety-five per cent. of the whole
male population of the United States of
America. But to-day the pervasive influence of Scotland has conquered America
as completely as Lord North failed to conquer it. I suppose there are about three
times as many first-class golf courses in the
United States of America as in any country
in the world. And more and more I observe
signs that the successful business men of
the United States are allowing themselves
this relaxation from their daily excitements.
More and more they seem to me in this re-

spect to be attaining a sane and equable philosophy of life.

I am not anxious in a sketch which is not intended to be controversial, except in one or two minor particulars, to involve myself in the great Protectionist controversy. I merely therefore note this fact: that it is evidently impossible to predicate of Protection that it is destructive of the economic fortunes of the nation which embraces its doctrines. For the prosperity of the United States is exuberant and phenomenal; and yet on my repeated visits to that country it so happens that I have never met a prominent business man who was a Free Trader. I have certainly met some men who thought that in some respect or other their tariff might be modified or altered. But I greatly doubt whether it would be possible to find among those who really count in the United States a dozen men who accept for their guidance the teachings of Cobden. I am well aware that it may be retorted (and I

have often made public admissions of this
fact) that the astounding natural resources
of the United States of America make it
impossible to derive from their experience
maxims valuable for the guidance of communities whose economic conditions are so
little comparable. But I note these circumstances, which I believe to be indisputable,
merely in order to make it plain that the
assumption that Free Trade is the best
policy for all countries at every stage in
their development is one that cannot be sustained. For the proposition that the whole
business world of the United States of
America is so blind to its own economic interests as not to know whether Free Trade
or Protection serves its interests best is a
paradox too wild to deserve or require disputation. In my mind, the requirements of
the domestic market in the United States
of America will for a long period of time,
perhaps twenty or thirty years, keep their
factories in busy employment. There is so

much wealth in the country, so much expansion and development, such self-confidence, that I see little prospect in the near future of any dependence on a large scale upon export markets for manufactured goods. And therefore I myself cannot see any prospect in the near future that the United States will be driven upon trading and industrial grounds to the conclusion that their own material interests demand a risky intervention into European politics.

The agricultural situation appears to me from the American standpoint to be more anxious. In this field America does at present require, and it may be will for a considerable time continue to require, the relief of foreign markets. And such markets will not emerge upon a paying basis until Europe and the world emerge from the aftermath of the War. There is unquestionably great discontent among the farmers of the United States. And this discontent may easily react fatally upon the fortunes of other of the great American political parties. For the agricultural population of America is extremely numerous, and politically not ill-organised. The difficulty of the Government in attempting to attract it politically is that it has nothing to offer which the farmers value. And so it happens, paradoxically enough, that the problem which we have to confront in this country, where we have unhappily sacrificed agriculture, is the same problem which must confront the Government at Washington, which cannot sacrifice it for years, and perhaps for generations.

In my judgment the political considerations which alone might induce the United States to take a more active and more responsible part in contributing to the problems of Europe are those which will or might arise from agricultural pressure in the field of politics.

To sum up my 'conclusions upon this

11

branch of the subject: The material advancement of the United States is stupendous. I can assign no limits to it. Not even the embarrassing possession of nearly all the gold of all the world is impeding or clogging the wheel of progress. I do not think that American economists and financiers have succeeded in exploiting to the full the extraordinary world opportunities which the post-war situation placed within their grasp; the explanation of this, in my judgment, is to be found in the fact that with all their shrewdness they lack something of the sophistication and age-long sagacity of Threadneedle Street. But no system of Protection will hold this people back from their onward advance in the race of ever-growing prosperity. They will or may intervene in European politics (a topic to be hereafter examined in this chapter, when they judge it in their interest so to do) but the only great field of national industry which affords a prospect that this conception may procure adoption is to be found in the precarious situation upon commercial conditions and partly in the great national business of agriculture.

(2) *The Negro Problem.*

This problem is admitted by most enlightened men in the United States of America to present one of the gravest which confronts their future. And indeed it is both historically strange and politically formidable. The white migration into this rich and unpeopled area wore down in days long since past the softness of the indigenous Indian. And having done so it was driven, having regard to the poverty of the available white population, to call into aid a servile population. And so resulted the slave trade. A new, virile, ineffaceable and very remarkable population became gradually established upon the American continent. It brought with it for a long time in servile conditions very extraordinary qualities. It

13

was superficially adaptable; it was physically immensely strong, resistant and resilient; and, what was to be even more important, it was attended by immense procreative fecundity. The problem, though difficult, was not unmanageable so long as the moral ideals of the United States tolerated the existence in its midst of a servile class. How long it could have been tolerated, how far it was ever tolerable, must be left to the historians of the United States to determine. Those who still vindicate (if any such still survive) the cause of the South may at least be permitted to make the claim that whatever concessions it was necessary to make in terms of morality in the excuse of their own system, they at least perfectly appreciated the ethical and social problems which must follow upon a substituted and more civilised conception. To-day the United States appear to be confronted by this problem: that more attractive industrial and social conditions are more and more tempting the negro population of the South to migrate northwards. The South had methods, right or wrong, which enabled it, even after the abolition of slavery, to cope with its Negro problem. I am not at all satisfied that the North, to whom this problem is novel, has either assimilated its realities or prepared itself to deal with the social consequences of its invasion. Almost like a horde of locusts the Negroes of the South are invading city after city of the rich and indiscriminating North. A whole area of Chicago—and not a disreputable one, fifteen years ago inhabited exclusively by a white population—has now been handed over in undisputed possession to the dark invader. And a large dealer in real estate who has spent his life carrying on that business in Chicago informed me that he could at present discern no limit to the invasion or to the encroachments involved in it over the adjacent tenements and streets of Chicago.

# AMERICA REVISITED

No one who has travelled much in the United States of America will ever speak unfavourably of the coloured population, taken as a whole. It has indeed many amiable, admirable and attractive qualities. All such travellers have in their minds grateful recollections of the friendly and courteous service, the unaffected cheerfulness, of the coloured attendants in railway cars. But the clear appreciation of the many attractive qualities of this cheerful and friendly people cannot blind one to the unbridgeable wall which the inscrutable purposes of Nature has placed between them and their white neighbours, and to the gravity and prominence of the problem which exists and must continue, when a strain so populous, so virile, so self-productive and so unassimilable, coexists on a continent, however vast, side by side with a white civilisation, which in many of these respects, however superior in others, cannot support its competition.

(3) *America and Europe.*

Upon this disputable subject it is necessary to write with reserve and to avoid generalisations. For opinion in the United States upon the present political situation in Europe is fluid, and, if one may be allowed a homely expression, "streaky." A large section of opinion unquestionably distrusts what it looks upon as French aggressiveness; and does not even hesitate to allege that one menace to the peace of Europe has been succeeded by another hardly less formidable. Others, on the contrary, take the view that Germany systematically, ever since the Treaty, has been avoiding her financial obligations thereunder, partly by deliberate deflation, partly by the wholesale transfer of securities to the United States and to other parts of the world. This school of thought holds that no method except such a one as that of M. Poincaré could bring the Germans to their senses; that Mr. Lloyd George was sentimental and ineffective in this matter; and that nothing but the iron hand would effectively secure such liquidation of German indebtedness as is actually practicable. I am inclined to think that these schools of thought would be equally balanced in the States were it not that the airy indifference of France in the matter of her indebtedness—a subject to which I shall hereafter refer more fully—had greatly prejudiced the general French position in the United States.

It is however possible to make certain broad statements with some confidence. In the first place, the citizens of the United States are now as always ready to support with generous warmth, upon however large a scale, private charities in relief of the sufferings of Europe. And indeed in this matter their noble exertions in Russia and their continued efforts to assist the victims of Turkish misrule fill shining pages in the history of international philanthropy. Nor indeed can any apparent limit be assigned

18

to the readiness of this generous and wealthy people to contribute in the field of private charities to the necessities of a stricken world.

But it must in the second place be made quite plain that Americans as a whole look upon the continued instability of European conditions with uneasiness, with distrust, and not without the attribution of a good deal of blame. The disordered conditions which they see existing everywhere in Europe lead them, in my judgment, more and more to congratulate themselves upon the immense national majority which repudiated the policy of President Wilson. And here we touch at once the very heart of the American attitude. President Wilson undertook responsibilities and made commitments the like of which no former President of the United States has ever attempted. He pledged the support of the United States of America to a League of Nations which possessed some measure of supersovereignty. He did this without the slightest real indication that the American nation was behind him in this attempt, and with many striking danger signals that it was not. When I visited the United States in 1918, I incurred much censure by emphasising in an address delivered to the New York Bar Association, and afterwards reprinted in "My American Visit" the points which led me very greatly to doubt whether the American nation ever would, or indeed ever ought to accept the League of Nations in the shape conceived by President Wilson. I was immediately assailed by the shrill idealists of two continents. I was told (quite untruthfully) that I was attacking President Wilson and his policy. I was told that I was an unimaginative materialist; and that I had done more harm by this one speech than good (if any) by all the other speeches I delivered in the United States of America. I can afford to dwell with some complacency upon this incident; but so far as I am aware, I was the only Englishman holding any public position who quite plainly discerned from the first that there was not the slightest prospect that the United States, when consulted, would accept the League of Nations. I made this speech very deliberately and after careful preparation; for I was very anxious to direct the attention of the people of America to the implications which were involved in the proposals of the President. For even then I saw quite plainly what an unfortunate situation would result if the President involved the world in a treaty which the Senate refused to ratify. I did not attack —I never have attacked—the general conceptions which underlie the scheme of the League of Nations. But I analysed with great care some of the more patent difficulties from the American point of view; and asked plainly and with some intentional cruelty whether this was the kind of League which American opinion was prepared to accept. I may add that I was completely undismayed by the stream of criticism which an address, the prescience of which has since been admitted by nearly all the leading papers of the United States of America, elicited among the sentimentalists of that day. And naturally I have never blamed the United States of America for rejecting these proposals the moment an opportunity for pronouncing upon them was afforded to the general body of citizens. But at the same time I must carefully guard myself from the criticism that I exonerate the people of America from a grave measure of responsibility for our present misfortunes. They are not themselves, for the reasons I have given, blameful for having rejected the Treaty of Versailles. In rejecting that Treaty they acted within the undoubted rights of a free people legally and even ethically. Had I myself possessed a vote in America I should certainly have recorded it against President Wilson. Their responsibility springs from quite another source, and it is a very deep one. They are the authors of their constitution, responsible for it, and to be judged by international misfortunes which are caused by its imperfections. Under that Constitution the President of the United States of America was legally empowered to go to Europe as the representative of the American people, armed with prestige, power, and rank to which no other negotiator could lay claim. For the President of the United States of America, during the period of his office, is armed with prerogative powers wielded by no potentate or minister in the world to-day. It is idle to say that Europe had plain warnings of the rumblings of discontent already audible in his own country. It was absolutely impossible to ask that they should make themselves the judges of future political developments in America. They were not only entitled—they were bound—to accept President Wilson as the authoritative

exponent of American views and American
wishes. A whisper even which could have
been construed as disrespectful to this great
man in the very zenith of his career would
have been generally and rightly resented all
over the States. We must throw our minds
back. This was the period of victorious in-
toxication. It was the day of the triumphant processions in London, in Paris, and
in Rome. Europe had no choice but to accept the workings and the implications of
the American constitution. And however
vivid may have been the apprehensions from
time to time entertained by those who nego-
tiated with President Wilson (and they
were very vivid) upon the ultimate outcome,
they could not, without risk of causing the
gravest offence in America, treat him in any
capacity except that of an exalted plenipo-
tentiary.

And so the long-drawn drama was played
out. The United States was pledged to become a member of the League of Nations

and to all the obligations which membership involved. They were equally pledged, jointly with Great Britain, to the Pact of mutual defence for the protection of France. Looking back, it is easy to see now how wholly alien both these obligations or sets of obligations were to the traditional foreign policy of the United States. But the confidence expressed by the President, in language so sonorous and so splendid, influenced even the most sceptical of his colleagues. And even those who still doubted realised the impossibility and even the indecency of challenging his credentials. It is not possible even now to judge how many of the misfortunes of Europe were directly due to this tragic and irrational optimism. The League of Nations has ever since been truncated. The Pact of Protection influenced and deflected much of the policy of Clémenceau; so that no one could state with confidence how far the whole Ruhr complication was produced by conditions which would never have arisen had the French been permitted to explore avenues which they reluctantly abandoned in exchange for the Pact. This and this alone is the claim which Europe has upon American help. It is a very real claim.

But I myself did not think it useful in the speeches which I delivered in the United States, some of which are reprinted in this volume, to make appeals *in misericordium* founded upon general claims of sentiment. The American nation is very just. The claims founded upon the considerations which I have just examined are unanswerable. It is to the more general realisation of these indisputable truths in America that we must look as the best hope of American national co-operation. But we should be blinding our eyes to indisputable facts if we did not recognise that the general policy of the United States is as clearly as it has ever been one of non-intervention in European affairs, except in so far as unquestioned American

interests render such intervention imperative. And the very impracticability of
President Wilson's proposals and the political hurricane which submerged them
have made it infinitely more difficult for a
reversal of that decision to be attempted by
any political party. The subject has become one of the great historic contentions
between parties which sometimes find it a
little difficult to raise clear and intelligibly
defined issues. I see no sign that the Democratic Party has the slightest intention of
compromising its electioneering prospects
by any real reversion to the proposals of
President Wilson. And the Republican
Party, which won so remarkable a victory
upon this issue, is showing considerable ner-
vousness even in relation to the proposed
International Court, modest as that proposal seems to those who formerly ranged
themselves for and against schemes so
grandiose.

My conclusion therefore upon this branch

of the subject is that the proposals of President Wilson and any comparable proposals have been not only decisively but for all time rejected by the American people. That people will never adhere to any League of Nations which imposes upon them not merely the degree but even the kind of responsibility which the President recommended. Nor will it ever pledge itself to any international undertaking resembling in the slightest degree the Pact of Protection which President Wilson believed himself authorised to offer to France. The United States will, in other words, continue to pursue their traditional policy. That policy is founded upon the conviction that the first duty of a nation is to its own nationals; that peace is better than war; that the geographical aloofness of the United States of America affords the Government of that country exceptional opportunities of protecting its citizens from the horrors of war; and that it is the duty of every American Government to mitigate the risks of international complications in every situation which does not directly menace a primary American interest.

But this people is as conscientious as it is cool in measuring the extent of any of its national responsibilities and I am certain that there exists already a great body of opinion, likely to become stronger rather than weaker, which in virtue of the considerations which I have attempted to urge, will more and more insist that the United States does labour under a great responsibility to Europe, and ought to contribute to its salvage by any methods which do not conflict with the principle of foreign policy which they regard as axiomatic.

(4) *America and Great Britain.*

This branch of the subject again requires to be examined with care and treated with delicacy. For here again generalisations are extremely misleading. It would be altogether wrong to underrate the appeal which British descent makes to a great section of the American people. In that strange amalgam of confluent populations, which has not yet made, though it will one day make, a homogeneous people, a certain satisfaction and even a certain pride is felt, not only by those millions whose ancestors sailed in the *Mayflower,* but also by those whose grandfathers or fathers have left in the last hundred years Liverpool or Birmingham or Manchester to seek new fortunes in a new world. And so in my travels in the States I was frequently touched by the numbers of those who came to me, claiming that their grandfather was a Liverpool man, or that their grandmother had been a Somersetshire girl.

We must not therefore ignore, though we must be careful not to exaggerate, the effect in America of an ancestry which those who possess it greatly, and rightly, value. Why indeed should we be guilty of the affectation of pretending that it is not a distinction to be sprung from the loins of these tiny islands, which for nearly a thousand years have flung their intellectual and political influence into the furthest corners of such a world as was known to each generation of its countrymen? But it is none the less true that every sentimental appeal has its reactions. None of the other European powers which has largely contributed to the population of the United States has in American eyes the unfortunate historical record of the British people. The disastrous effects produced by King George III and Lord North are even now (incredible as it may appear) hardly exhausted. Indeed, much of the sympathy of the United States with Ireland sprang from a vague conviction that Ireland had for centuries been treated much as Lord North tried to treat the American Colonies. The influence of historical textbooks in the public schools of America, in this connection, has frequently been ex-plained. Their authors talk much and quite justifiably of Lord North and the King. They give less prominence to the noble and generous eloquence of Lord Chatham and Mr. Burke. The folly of which those were guilty who were at that time unhappily in control of the destinies of Great Britain ought not to blind our eyes to the fact that even in that tragic quarrel there were two sides. The main burden of the defence of the American Colonies, so far as those Colonies were menaced—as they constantly were—by European powers, fell upon Great Britain. It was unquestionably right that these Colonies should make some contribution to an Imperial expenditure without which they must incontestably have fallen the victims of a European power which would certainly not have treated them better than Great Britain. But the difficulty was that the Colonies never could agree, and never would agree, upon the proportion which they ought to pay. "No representation, no taxation" has a noble sound; but the consequences are less noble when you really mean that you do not desire representation and cannot agree among yourselves to contribute anything to the taxation. This nevertheless was the historical truth of the crisis which produced the struggle for independence. These considerations do not of course involve any defence of the tactless blundering and unstatesmanlike handling of the situation by the British Government. A larger vision, more sympathetic imagination, and more generous patience would undoubtedly have afforded the means of an accommodation with men who at that time were almost all of our own blood, were in the main reasonable and capable of compromise, and who certainly did not desire to carry an unhappy quarrel to extremities. But the controversy is now so old, and it has become so completely a matter for the historian, that an Englishman is entitled to pray in aid of the complete and repeatedly

expressed inability of the Colonies to agree
either upon the formula or substance of
their contribution to the Imperial expenditure. Almost every one at that time blundered. We blundered most of all. The most
unfortunate element in ancient historical
quarrels is that among peoples of tenacious
memories their consequences last so long.
And it would, in my judgment, be a mistake
even to-day to imagine that this age-long
bitterness has exhausted its capacity for
mischief.

But it must at the same time be realised
that there is much in our temperament, our
civilisation and our history, which is deeply
admired in the United States. Our general
outlook upon the politics of the world and
upon the greatest problems of contemporary
humanity is the same. We each have so
much that neither wants any more. The
deepest interests of both countries require
peace and tranquillity. Neither is in any
circumstances capable of an aggressive war.

In both countries there exist noble humanitarian forces which Imperial Germany never could have understood, and which no statesman or military caste could ever control, inflexibly opposed to bloodshed if bloodshed can be avoided without disloyalty to national safety and national existence. And it may therefore be proudly claimed that however powerful at a given moment may be the forces which cherish no special liking for Great Britain, there will always be found in balanced equipoise great sections of the population which either from heredity, or from political or intellectual sympathy, earnestly desire to maintain friendly and even cordial relations with this country.

This subject cannot be dismissed without noticing the numerical strength with which the present population of the United States has been recruited from the rest of the world, by an enormous infusion of Irish, German, Italian, French, Scandinavian and other elements.

# AMERICA REVISITED

Statistics make it plain how obsolete is the talk that blood is thicker than water. Indeed, without incurring the charge of snobbishness, we may perhaps make it plain that we have little claim to pose as the cousins of that great family which, as I have already pointed out, enjoys to-day the hegemony in the New York directory.

The conditions of our friendship with the United States of America may be summarised in a rather different way:

Many of their citizens have inherited our blood and share the traditions of the England of Shakespeare and Milton. Many others are in broad agreement with our outlook upon world affairs. Almost all educated Americans, whether our friends or not, have a generous admiration for the history, achievement and traditions of a country so small, of which the population during that achievement has been relatively so inconsiderable. But these, and these alone, are the considerations which we must

36

treat as actual, and as ever in human affairs, that which is actual is on the whole more important than that which is sentimental.

(5) *The United States and Ireland.*

The greatest triumph which British statesmanship has achieved during the last hundred years in its diplomatic relations with the United States is unquestionably to be found in the Irish Settlement. The emigration from Ireland to America during the last hundred years has been astounding in its exuberance. And nearly all that emigration has proceeded, not from the North, but from the South. The result has been that ninety per cent. of Irish emigration to America has consisted of the bitterest enemies of this country. The Irishman has many qualities, some very attractive, some less attractive. But no one has ever disputed that if he inherits a quarrel which passionately engages his feelings, he will transmit it more tenaciously from father to son than any islander has ever succeeded in doing since the happiest days of Corsica. And by universal consent, Irishmen possess, if not the highest form of political cleverness, at least political adaptability and resources of a very unusual character. Thus it came about for many years that a powerful section of the population of the United States of America capable of discipline, willing to undertake the labours without which successful political organisation is impossible, was bitterly and irreconcilably opposed to the interests of Great Britain. And being ourselves human and not altogether inexperienced in politics, we must take note of the reactions of this state of affairs upon American politics. The Irish vote, perfectly organised, never vacillating, sure of itself, became at recurrent intervals of great and even of decisive importance in American politics. So those who in these Islands desired a warm and friendly relationship with

America found themselves in this difficult situation, that a great, active, and very vocal section in American political life was utterly irreconcilable and would vote for any party which encouraged them to ventilate grievances ancient and bitter, but by no means always unjust, against Great Britain.

We were often exhorted in old days by true American friends to set our house in order. Our advisers had not always studied the strange and tragic history of Ireland. Had that country been a single and homogeneous community, no difficulty could or would have arisen. But unhappily for its solution, our ancestors, hundreds of years ago, had as a matter of deliberate policy planted Scotch and English settlers in the north of Ireland. For hundreds of years these men had afforded an equipoise, relied upon by an unbroken series of British Governments, against repeated attempts in the direction of secession. They preserved their dour and individual character as jealously as did the wholly different population of the South. The differences between the two populations were intensified by religious cleavages which were tenacious, fanatical and almost mediæval. It was as certain as anything in the world has ever been certain that the attempt compulsorily to place the North of Ireland under the South, as numerically they must have been in a Parliament sitting at Dublin, would have produced a bloody civil war. Home Rule therefore as presented by Mr. Gladstone and his successors was impracticable and never could have succeeded, because it drew no distinction between the evidently separable conditions of the North and of the South. I admit most fully that I myself proceeded with Lord Carson to great lengths—and would even have proceeded to greater—in order to prevent the forcible inclusion of the Northern provinces in a Parliament sitting at Dublin. But it is not necessary to attempt a lengthy argument for the justification of

that which was then said and done. For
four successive Prime Ministers—Mr. Asquith, Mr. Lloyd George, Mr. Bonar Law
and Mr. Baldwin—have concurred in the
view which we then formed, and which was
the justification of our actions, that Ulster
could never be coerced, even if she might
ultimately be persuaded to become part of
a larger Irish polity. And it may be added
with some confidence that it is extremely unlikely that the fifth Prime Minister, Mr.
Ramsay MacDonald, will take a different
view. It is therefore sufficient for us in our
justification to make it plain that that
against which we contended is now universally admitted to have been wrong and impracticable; it is not disputed that if actually attempted it would have led to civil
war; we on our part are content to state our
case in the terms that an extreme measure
of resistance in speech and even in act may
be justified in the case of those who were re-
sisting a policy now universally admitted to

have been unfair, impracticable and certainly productive of civil war.

But it was hardly reasonable to expect that the subtler sides of this controversy should have been completely understood in the United States, where indeed all the missionary talk was upon one side. And therefore it happened that for fifty or sixty years the relations between this country and America were embittered by an open sore. Many complaints were made in 1914 of the slowness of the United States to appreciate the ethical aspects of the Allied cause. To those who understand politics it may have appeared almost a sufficient explanation (though there were others) that the Irish population in the United States of America amounted to not less than four million persons born in Ireland and their children and that the German population, in a similar category, in the United States amounted to over seven million. The figures for the population of Irish and German extraction

are not available, but if one considers the
continuous absorption of immigrants of both
these races during the last century some idea
of their relative racial influence may be ap-
prehended. He was indeed an optimist who
expected that the cultivated opinion of the
West, the generous friendship of those who
still felt themselves to be of our kin, could
sweep away within a short period of time
forces at once so powerful and so imper-
vious to reason and to sentiment.

The first glimmer of hope in this matter
was disclosed when there succeeded to the
campaign of destruction and assassination
the hope of a settlement by conference. Nor
in the early stages was the hope either considerable or generally entertained by those
who took part in that conference. But as
its discussion proceeded it became plain that
Ireland was represented by two remarkable
though very widely different men. I had
myself gone into the conference without any
real hope that it could be brought to a suc-

43

cessful conclusion. But the personalities of
Mr. Arthur Griffith and Mr. Mike Collins
gradually and almost insensibly altered my
view, and so, painfully, uncertainly, doubt-
fully, we groped our way to a solution which
I believe beyond doubt will be pronounced
by history to be the greatest effort of statecraft in the whole history of the relations,
first between Great Britain and Ireland;
and secondly between Great Britain and the
United States. Of this at least I satisfied
myself by constant enquiry in almost every
centre of population in America which I
visited. There is no longer an Irish Party
which is important so long as it depends
upon any Irish grievances. As between
President Cosgrave and Mr. De Valera, the
latter is almost without an adherent. You
cannot in any great city in the United States
collect a representative audience of American citizens to recreate the Irish issue. And
if here and there you find sporadically distributed in the cities where the Irish cause

was once so strong an adherent of De Valera, you will always find that these men have all their lives been implacable enemies of Great Britain, and that rather than abandon this pleasurable habit of mind they are content to become the followers even of a De Valera.

The settlement of this ancient controversy, which we happily attained and which the energy and courage of President Cosgrave and his friends is daily making more successful, has done more to remove controversy and the risk of it between the United States and this country than any other single cause except their sacred association in the Great War.

My summary upon this part of my examination is that the kindness and generosity and hospitality of American hosts to American guests is greater than ever it was; that no added difference has developed, or as far as I can see is likely to develop, between the two countries in the near future; and that the most bitter, awkward and durable cause

45

of discord has been removed by the Great
Irish Settlement.

(6) *The Social Life of America To-day.*

The observations which I have to make
upon this attractive subject must be carefully separated from those which I shall
have to offer in a separate chapter under
the heading of "Prohibition." The two
topics are indeed, as may be supposed,
not unrelated; but different considerations
arise, and I find it on the whole more convenient to deal with the two topics sepa-
rately.

It cannot be doubted that for rich people
America is one of the most delightful countries in the world in which to live. The climate is indeed over a large extent of its surface harsh and extreme; but so great is the
extent of that surface that those who can afford the means of locomotion can always
vary their climate at any period of the year.
Such travelling activities are not of course

46

within the range of all. But nevertheless an extraordinary proportion of the amenities of life is open to, and is enjoyed by, the working classes. A significant illustration of this fact may be given. There are more motor cars in the State of New York than there are in the whole of Great Britain. Six out of ten workingmen own either a Ford or some kind of a "Flivver." I myself saw a great building in process of construction in the environs of Chicago around which sixty-eight small motor cars were waiting to carry sixty-eight artisans home after their day's work. There is consequently no jealousy in the United States based upon the possession of motor cars as being a special privilege of the rich. But the immense accumulation of cars in the hands of the whole population is producing a traffic problem to which the most experienced minds in the United States see no answer. In fact, one of the greatest authorities in New York told me that, while many disagreed with him, he was himself convinced that the New York problem would never be manageable until they had constructed over the busy parts of the city a complete duplicated overhead system of roads. I cross-examined him as to the mammoth cost that would be involved in such a scheme. His estimate exceeded even my expectations. But he nevertheless assured me on the authority of one of the greatest transport experts in New York City, that it was, in his judgment, inevitable that such an enterprise must come. The problem in Chicago was hardly less striking. A great merchant in that city who lived in the suburbs told me that he always left his car three miles from his office and took his chance of a street car or a taxicab. Of all the social changes which I observed in the United States after five years' absence the immense increase in the number of automobiles was incomparably the most striking.

With this stupendous growth in material prosperity which has taken place in ten years there has been afforded everywhere greater opportunity of indulging those generous and hospitable impulses which Englishmen have always recorded of their visits to the States. If a visitor is liked he will be passed on his travels from one delightful companion to another with a letter which makes it unnecessary to seek other friends in that particular city.

And at last, as I have already pointed out, the United States are beginning to realise that life is short, health vital, dollars incapable of transfer to the next world, and that therefore there is much to be said for a reasonable enjoyment of life in this. And so on the Eastern coast all sections of society have carried lawn tennis to a scale of general practice which seems likely to retain for long the championship of the world. And so no self-respecting "burgh" counts itself anything at all unless it has established a golf course and a professional (generally a Scotchman), both of whom are just a little better than those of its nearest rival.

On the life of its great universities, some of which I had the opportunity of visiting, I cannot speak without deep admiration. The spirit and the *esprit de corps* are as great as in any known to us. And even though it sound egotistic to make the claim, I must as an Englishman be allowed to say their athletic associations have captured and retain all that is best of our public-school traditions.

I have been often asked whether in my widely spread travels I detected many fundamental differences between West, Middle West and East. A stranger is never especially sensitive to such differences. I found in all the great cities charming, cultivated and kindly people. I did further discover, not without amusement, that there was a general resentment in the Middle West against the portraiture of their lives which is contained in Mr. Sinclair Lewis' clever books. I forget now and am writing without books of reference, but I believe that seven Greek cities compete for the honour of having given birth to the great Homer. I am able confidently to state that at least seventy "burghs" are contending that they have nothing to do with either Main Street or Babbitt's City.

I have already suggested that it is impossible to discuss with any completeness the contemporary social life of the United States without a careful and analytical study of the effect of Prohibition upon that life, and to that task, with the caution becoming to a stranger, I shall address myself in the next chapter.

# CHAPTER II

THE importance and the vividness of the controversy which Prohibition excites in the United States to-day is imperfectly exhibited in their Press. I was on my recent visit for nearly three months in the United States. I can hardly recall one single meal in which the topic of Prohibition was successfully avoided. No account, however superficial and fugitive, of a visit to America would be complete without an attempt to examine and collate the results of the most interesting social experiment which any country in the world still calling itself free has ever made. Five years ago, observing movements and tendencies, I wrote in "My 'American Visit" the following sentence:

"The forces deploying for this great so-

cial antagonism are not unequally matched.
It will be interesting to study the final result
of their collision."

Since then Prohibition has gained its victory in the United States, has conquered territory which it has since proved unable to
hold in the Dominion of Canada, and has
afforded a sufficient period of time for
analysis and criticism.

The attack upon alcohol was of course one
of the most remarkable that any country has
ever attempted. This drug has been used
in one form or another almost from the twilight of the human race. Its effects were
no doubt unfavourably illustrated on more
than one occasion in the Old Testament.
And names even as respectable as those of
Noah and King David may be without un-
reasonableness, thanks to the care and
frankness of the Old Testament chroniclers,
enlisted on behalf of a teetotal argument.

The plain truth appears to be that alcohol
used in moderation is a very agreeable addi-

tion to the amenities of life. I still remember the late Lord Halsbury, at a dinner which I gave when Lord Chancellor, to the judges of Belgium, drinking two glasses of champagne and a glass of port in his ninety-seventh year. It is equally true that the abuse of alcohol has through the ages encouraged vice, promoted crime, and induced the ruin, moral and physical, of weak persons. But it is quite certain that the controversy will continue, because it is founded upon fundamental disparities of temperament in human nature. There will always be those who will sing with Fitzgerald:

Ah, fill the Cup:—what boots it to repeat
How Time is slipping underneath our Feet:
Unborn TO-MORROW and dead YESTERDAY,
Why fret about them if TO-DAY be sweet!

There will always be those who, if assailed by scriptural argument, will recall that the Psalmist indulgently spoke of "wine that makes glad the mind of man"; and that our

# PROHIBITION

Lord turned water into wine. This particular miracle has always seemed to me to make it impossible to found any Prohibitionist movement upon a religious basis. For the very slight allusions I have made to two deplorable cases of excess in the Old Testament make it certain that at the moment when a divine miracle deliberately converted water into wine, the perils, the improprieties and even the indecencies which are apt to accompany alcoholic excess were almost as clearly appreciated as they are to-day.

Those who found themselves upon the literal or actual inspiration either of the New Testament or of the Old in these matters must, if they be candid, admit that the argument requires to be founded upon modern considerations of expediency rather than upon eternal principles of right.

The historical development of Prohibition in the United States requires some slight examination. There have for a long period of time been "dry" States, particularly in the South, but the drought was humanely, considerately and scientifically conceived in the interests of the negro population. There was, it is true, a considerable body of opinion in the United States which over a long period of time struggled in the interests of compulsory teetotalism. But studying as carefully as I can the results of these efforts and expressing my opinion with the hesitation proper to a stranger, I cannot reach the conclusion that until the War these movements had made great progress or were within reach of success. The conditions produced by the War in the United States of America were remarkable. The very fact that the United States came late into a war, of which, when once it was embraced, they realised and expressed in eloquent terms the moral justice, led perhaps to a higher degree of sentimentalism than was observable in any other of the self-governing Allies. The Prohibition Party in America was astute to observe the gains which might be made by a cause hitherto unsuccessful if it were founded upon an appeal which was so congruous with the earnest patriotism of the moment. And accordingly it was put forward everywhere where patriotic Americans met that the evils of alcohol were clogging and impeding the national effort. And this argument was, I am told, very powerfully put forward by many who made no specially noticeable contribution to the national effort.

But even so, making full allowance for the extent to which the sentiment of the country could be exploited by a patriotic even if an illogical appeal, I doubt greatly whether the campaign would have succeeded if two quite different sets of conditions had not converged to forward its career.

In the first place, the condition and character of the saloons in the great cities of America were on the whole one of the great scandals of the world. Every responsible American was thoroughly ashamed of them.

And yet they were extremely powerful when merely confronted by local, municipal, or even by State assault. It seemed to many—politics being what they are—that no movement short of a national movement could possibly destroy the saloons. And it appeared to many reasonable men that if there were no other way of smashing the saloons except that of national prohibition, it might almost be worth while to run the risk of employing this particular dynamite.

And in the second place it must be carefully noticed that the temperance movement in the United States never attained practical results, and probably, in spite of the sentimentalism induced by the War, never would have attained practical results, if it had not been reinforced by a powerful impetus proceeding from the great employers of labour. In other words, the movement, so long as it was a moral movement, never attained to any great measure of success. The War increased the sentimental forces behind it. And when the financiers and the capitalists, in the interests of the efficiency of labour, threw their influence upon the same side, the combination so aggregated became the most formidable which any country has ever enlisted in the cause of Prohibition.

The methods of the reformers and their tactics were extremely ingenious. They were adopted with an exact knowledge of the rigid quality which appertains to the Constitution and to its authorised amendments. And the change so made, prodigious in its consequences, as yet incalculable in its reactions, can only be disturbed by a combination of chances and opportunities of the reverse kind which is extremely unlikely to occur.

It is evident that two questions require an honest and informed answer before one can reach even a provisional conclusion upon this most difficult problem.

(1) Has it on the whole succeeded in at-

taining its professed object, namely, that of stamping out the sale, distribution, transportation, and consumption of alcoholic liquor?

(2) If it has not so succeeded, what are the consequences of that failure: and what inferences are to be drawn from that failure in relation to the moral aim attempted?

Let me attempt to examine in general terms the answer which must, I think, be made almost without risk of controversy to the first of these questions. It must be made in general terms because a grateful guest entertained by kind hosts under difficult circumstances may be excused for the employment of some slight reticence. But this may be plainly said by me—because it is everywhere plainly said in the United States— that this is a law which plainly operates in favour of the rich and plainly operates against the poor. It is, I think on the whole, true that the working classes of the United States do better work under Prohibition

than they did before. Larger numbers of
them return to work on Monday morning.
Such an arrangement is doubtless admirable
from the point of view of an employer of
labour, who had his own cellar laid down
upon a munificent scale in the days before
Prohibition, and who has nothing to lose
and everything to gain by the enforced
sobriety of his employees. But while I
am not disposed to dispute the solid gain
which has accrued to industrial efficiency
from Prohibition, even here a sombre and
different picture must be drawn. It is not
given to all men, even to workingmen, to
withdraw themselves absolutely from the attraction of alcohol, just as it is not given to
all rich men. And even during the short
time in which I was in the United States,
I read of thirty-four different cases in which
poor men, who had no cellars, had perished
by drinking poisoned alcohol. So great indeed was the alarm that was created by
these repeated and most tragic casualties

that in many towns the existing public agencies for determining the purity of substances submitted to them had been enormously expanded in order to deal with the submission for test and certification of alcohol illegally obtained, or illegally manufactured, which the consumer would not accept until it was vouched for by an analyst.

I apply myself now to the broad question: Has or has not Prohibition expelled alcohol from the United States? The answer is notorious. It unquestionably has not. It is quite true that there are many small towns, and many more villages, where it is impossible to obtain alcohol. But in my journeys through the towns, where I always in a spirit of social curiosity asked the question, I was invariably informed that Prohibition was not very strictly enforced there, but that if you went to another town (whose name was obligingly given) you would there find that its full enforcement was effective. A practical commentary upon the success of the United States' authorities in excluding alcohol is to be found in the fact that the best Scotch whisky was only sixpence a bottle dearer in New York than in Montreal. And this was not supplied through dangerous channels but by a most respected bootlegger who to my knowledge belonged to at least one good club in New York.

The real truth is that when you have a population of over one hundred millions, of whom at least some millions desire to enjoy a form of refreshment which is exhilarating, and which many people have enjoyed since the dawn of the world; when that country has thousands of miles of boundary, from the Dominion of Canada in the North to Mexico in the South; when it is additionally handicapped by having I know not how many thousand miles of maritime access; when the trade is profitable beyond the dreams of avarice; no Government, however resolute, however wealthy, however equipped, could ever enforce such an exclusion. Spasmodic efforts are made from time to time. Meetings of governors are convened. Perhaps all the governors are not unanimous. The police force of a great city is completely and publicly purged. But nothing very effective is done. Nor indeed could anything very effective be conceived. New York State has already formally withdrawn its own very great resources from any attempt to assist the Federal authorities to enforce the law of Prohibition. I am told that other States are contemplating or have already adopted similar action.

Nor must it be assumed that the fundamental difficulties in the enforcement of Prohibition proceed entirely from the difficulties of intercepting smuggled alcohol. The very resources of Nature are enlisted against him who would dry up the gifts of Nature. A chemist can produce alcohol by boring a small hole in a ripe apple and exposing it to the sun's rays for a sufficient period. Home-brewed beers of excellent quality—for I have tasted them—are common on the farms of the Middle West; though I think that on the whole the labourers drink less of them than the farmers do. Applejack, a potent liqueur stronger than old brandy, is a common subject of rural production.

But the most singular illustration of all is furnished by the case of California. When it became known that Prohibition was certain to succeed, a most disastrous slump immediately occurred in the vineyards of California. These were quoted and sold at about forty per cent. of their pre-war values. And indeed everybody assumed that in the austere régime which was to reform American life these vineyards had exhausted alike their moral and material utility. But what has happened since? The same lands are being sold to-day—and not for the purposes of growing grain—at a higher price than they were sold for in the year before Prohibition became a law of the land. There is no reason to suppose that the American appetite for grapes as such has greatly increased in the interval. The plain and universally admitted truth is that the Californian grapes are being distributed all over the continent for the purposes of private wine presses. And I myself met five different American citizens of the highest position and respectability—men of whom any country might be proud—who told me that they imported grapes from California and wine makers from Italy, in order that their respective ages might not be compelled to depart, by what they regarded as an intolerant tyranny, from lifelong habits.

I summarise therefore the answer to the first question which I have proposed by saying: (1) That nearly every very rich man in the United States has a pre-Prohibition cellar which will last him for many years. (2) That no poor man has such a cellar. (3) That the rich man can reinforce his supply because he can afford to pay an absolutely reliable bootlegger. (4) That the poor man, if he decides to drink, must take terrible risks, because the kind of bootlegger open to him is less expensive and less discriminating. (5) That apart from bootlegging and smuggling, the consumption of alcohol upon an immense scale takes place in the United States of America. (6) It naturally happens that the proceeds of that consumption inures almost entirely to those who have the wit to contrive it and the resources to establish it. (7) That no one who is careful, prudent and equipped with money need fail to obtain reliable alcohol at a comparatively reasonable price in any great city in the United States of America to-day.

It remains now to consider the second question which I proposed, viz., What are the consequences of the failure at present universally admitted; and what inferences are to be drawn from that failure in relation to the moral aim attempted? Although the failure is almost universally conceded, it must not therefore be assumed that in the peculiar circumstances which exist in the United States the Prohibition Act will be repealed. Nothing appears to me less likely. It is indeed true that there exists a considerable movement in favour of allowing the consumption of light wines and beers. Such a change is no doubt recommended to those who advocate it by the fact that it could be effected by a modification in the schedule of the Volstead Act without undertaking the almost impossible task of amending, in the cumbrous method which alone is possible, the Constitution. But I do not think that even this slight modification is likely to be attempted. In the first place no political party quite dares to embark upon deep waters of controversy upon each side of which so many powerful and immeasurable forces are ranged. I have, for instance, little doubt that the overwhelming majority of American women is opposed to any modification of the existing law. Such an admission does not, of course, conclude the matter; for I have never been prepared to admit that a majority of women ought to be allowed to impose, or could indeed in the long run succeed in imposing, their views upon a powerful minority of unconvinced men. But at the same time I am concerned with the political prospects. And it appears to me that neither of the great parties in the States is prepared to jeopardise its prospects without greater assurance than is at present available that on balance they would gain more than they lost by embracing the cause of modification or repeal. Such a time may come. It has not come yet.

And in the second place I do not expect to see the smaller mitigation of the present austere system adopted for another reason. The relief would no doubt be considerable. It would diminish unquestionably the numbers of those who resolutely and openly break the existing law. It would not end or even much diminish the existing scandals of smuggling and bootlegging. For that which to-day is imported by these methods is neither beer nor light wine. Both beer and light wine are, as I have shown, manufactured upon a considerable scale already. And both are too bulky to be the profitable subject matter for bootlegging. The plain fact is that in the United States, as in every civilised country in the world, millions of citizens desire to drink spirits. They resent absolutely a law which in their opinion is a gross usurpation upon the domain of private conscience. And they have not the slightest intention of acquiescing in the present system or of abating any of the rights which they would enjoy if they were citizens either of Great Britain or of France. It seems to me for these reasons unlikely that any Party powerful enough to afford the promise of success will propose to render legal the sale of beer and light wines. If there were any prospect that such a modification would end the problems and the scandals of the existing system, the matter might possibly, if not certainly, require a different decision. But there is no such prospect; and I adhere to the opinion above expressed.

It is proper now to examine the larger question: What is the prospect that Prohibition will *in toto* be repealed, and that the United States will now or hereafter regain in this respect the social freedom which is enjoyed by every country in the world?

We cannot of course reason from the experience of the Dominion of Canada. That country indeed succumbed, except where the sturdy common sense of the French population of Quebec proved an obstacle too strong for conquest by the wave of emotionalism which swept over the United States. But it has been changing its mind ever since and has given in nearly every province practical expression to these changes. Indeed, the comfortable material advantages afforded to a population where alcohol can be obtained by contiguity, over a boundary of

71

thousands of miles, with an infinite and thirsty population, where it can not be procured, have produced the result which any reasonable man would have expected. Montreal, for instance, has become a very favourite place for long week-end visits by citizens of the United States. And the experience of Montreal is being repeated on a smaller scale in every Canadian centre, urban or rural, which affords the prospect of a pleasurable and refreshing visit. I have already attempted to make it plain that the decisive causes which fastened Prohibition upon the United States were not moral, but economic and commercial. It is ironical to discover that the causes which are leading to its failure in the Dominion are equally not moral but economic and financial.

The system which prevails in most parts of the Dominion is that of sale by the Government. Wine indeed, including champagne and beer, can be obtained at any restaurant or hotel. Spirits can only be obtained at a Government shop. Only one bottle is allowed upon a single visit. But the visitor, if his need be great, is permitted to repeat his visit with the same fruitful consequence. So that if a man wants six bottles of whisky he must send his servant six times to the Government shop. The method is perhaps a little more clumsy, but the result ultimately obtained is not very distinguishable from the easy system to which we are accustomed at home.

So much money has been made in the Dominion of Canada, directly and indirectly, as the result of Prohibition in the States, that financial conditions in the only great province which still remains dry are imperiously suggesting a change in the present law. I am inclined to believe that almost by the time these words appear in print it will be found that the whole of the Dominion of Canada has recoiled from this bizarre experiment.

But it is not so easy for the United States

of America to recoil. Their Constitution, as is made plain in a speech which I reprint later in this volume, cannot so easily be modified. Prohibition has become a part of the Constitutional Law of the United States and has accordingly taken its place in that adamant, cast-iron surrounding in which so many artificial obstacles are opposed to the path of the reformer. The arguments hitherto employed in dealing with the suggested legitimation of the sale of light wines and beer apply *a fortiori* to a change infinitely more difficult to bring about and certain to attract a more violent and widely spread antagonism. And the political difficulties, already great, are enormously increased by a very singular circumstance. Reference has already been made in this chapter to that new American industry, viz., bootlegging. The resources of that industry, its ingenuity, its ramifications, its influence and its organisation are little if at all understood in this country; I doubt even whether they are completely appreciated in the United States. And for the first time in the history of any country the whole influence of the drink trade—now an illegitimate, not a legitimate trade—is thrown upon the side of fanatical teetotalism. I was indeed informed, and upon credible authority, that many bootleggers' cheques, decorously masked of course, help to swell the funds of Prohibition. Could a situation more savagely ironical be conceived? A system was imposed upon vast numbers of American citizens—whether a majority or a minority matters in this connection not at all—which they repel as tyrannous. The drink trade, discerning as they believe in these proposals the knell of doom, resisted them, but vainly, in all its organised strength. The result is that the drink trade of to-day is enthroned in greater strength and hardly less wealth than before, though its activities have been driven to illegitimate and subterranean channels. And just because the profits of this trade are so stupendous those who carry it on prefer the existing system, with all its risks, to the doubtful chance of reversion to the old practice. And for this reason they are the most formidable, if they are the most silent allies of prohibition in the United States of America.

It remains to be asked what inferences ought to be drawn from a failure which I have attempted to establish and shall hereafter venture to assume, upon the moral aims attempted.

I have already made it plain that there exists some country districts and some unsophisticated towns in which the difficulty of obtaining alcohol has no doubt effectively ended the alcohol habit. In such places it is no doubt true that the new generation will grow up screened, as long as it dwells where it was born, from a penetrating temptation, which strong men have generally resisted, but before which weaklings have frequently succumbed. It may be conceded that this

76

gain—so far as it is a gain—may be set plainly upon one side of the account. And let it equally be conceded that an inference of greater sobriety among the working classes may be drawn from the fuller attendance which the wages sheets in industrial concerns disclose on Monday mornings. Let it be admitted further that the Savings Bank deposits have increased in the period under consideration (although indeed the growing prosperity of the whole country affords in itself no small explanation of such an increase). But when all these admissions are made, there remains a powerful number of overwhelming considerations upon the other side.

The American nation has in the main always been admirably law-abiding. The framers of their Constitution and their High Judges perceived with unswerving clearness of vision that respect for law is the very foundation of civilisation. And a nation cannot respect the law in streaks.

For it is one majestic whole. Its reputation, its binding force, the reverence which citizens entertain for it, depend, not upon one out of the thousand angular aspects; they depend and always will depend upon the general recognition that *"It is the Law and because it is, the Law must be obeyed."* You can no more attempt reverence for the law as a whole while segregating one department from that whole as foolish, indefensible and therefore violable, than you can say of a citizen that he is a man of the most admirable moral character, but that he unfortunately suffers from occasional homicidal impulses.

Those who forced Prohibition upon the American people did it with the full knowledge that millions of their fellow-countrymen would repel it as a tyrannous injustice. What is the consequence? In every large city the law is openly violated. Citizens of the highest consequence, who have never violated any other law, openly and even smilingly admit that they recognise no obligation under this law. Some restaurants in large cities place alcohol upon their tables with the same openness as is to be observed at the Carlton Restaurant. Men and women of the highest position openly use the expression "my bootlegger." It is indeed a notorious fact that the exports of Scotch whisky from one great English house to the United States of America have actually increased since the adoption of Prohibition.

Surely the results as they have so far emerged from this experiment justify the conclusion that where one is dealing with self-relating actions, the only moral conquests which are either valuable or attainable are those which are gained upon conscience through conviction; and that a law which intolerantly imposes upon adult citizens an abstinence which they dislike, by prescriptions which they consider tyrannous, can never effect a permanent improvement in human morals.

79

# CHAPTER III

## THE DOMINION OF CANADA

It is a long-established and kindly custom of the American Bar Association to invite each year an English judge, or an eminent member of the English Bar, to deliver an address on some legal or quasi-legal subject at their annual meeting. The guest is entertained with the generosity and completeness which the American nation so thoroughly understands. I myself was met in New York by Mr. Paul D. Cravath, of the American Bar, who took our party at once into a private car, the manifold comforts of which we never relinquished till we reached Montreal.

By a custom equally convenient and pleasant, it is the habit of the Canadian Bar Association to invite the same guest, after his

American speech, to address its members upon some other subject. A memorable precedent is being set in the present year, by which the British and Canadian Bars, acting as joint hosts, are entertaining in London some eight hundred members of the American Bar. The occasion is not only social but formal; for the American Bar Association, after dealing upon American soil with its purely domestic problems, will actually resume its session for the purposes of public legal discussion, in London. The lawyers of London, barristers and solicitors alike, will therefore be afforded the opportunity of showing, by the exchange of willing hospitality, that those of their members who have been the guests of American lawyers across the ocean have failed neither to realise nor to recount the warmth of their welcome.

And indeed the conception is one to strike the coldest imagination. Centuries after the *Mayflower* sailed, the flower of the American Bar, realising *Melius est petere fontes quam sectari rivulos,* revisits, as valued guests, the historic origins of Anglo-Saxon jurisprudence.

In the Dominion we received kindness as distinguished as in the United States. The generosity of Sir Henry Thornton, Chairman of the Canadian National Line, placed at our disposal a splendid car for the whole journey from Montreal to Vancouver. And the late Lord Shaughnessy kindly allowed the car which made the outward journey upon the National Company's line to return —varying the scenery—by the Canadian Pacific.

This was the first time I had travelled further west than Winnipeg; the opportunity therefore of seeing this vast country almost from seaboard to seaboard was specially valuable. I addressed in every large city which I visited one or more meetings upon subjects of Imperial interest. I was naturally thrown in contact with many leading men in the Dominion, and I had therefore some opportunity of learning their views upon the general conditions, economic and political, which prevail in Canada today.

My last visit had been paid in 1918, when Canada was as intensely absorbed in her war effort as we at home. And equally, of course, the high emotion of those terrible days had disappeared, and, as is intelligible, the less sophisticated community has suffered less in mental and material reaction than our older civilisation. Indeed, the superficial observer might travel over a considerable distance in the Dominion without even discovering that it had recently played a triumphant part, involving the loss of thousands of lives, in the great World War.

I think that on the whole optimism prevails in relation to the business future. Generalisations are always difficult, but of all those interested in commerce with whom

I discussed the matter, I only record one or two pessimists. And indeed, gloom of long duration is difficult to reconcile with the possession of a land of such incalculable promise. It is worth making the journey if only to see, league after league, the immense grainfields of the Middle West. And the mineral wealth of Canada will certainly not contribute less to her ultimate resources. For it is hardly an exaggeration to say, taking the Dominion as a whole, that even in likely areas the surface, in relation to that stupendous whole, has hardly yet been scratched.

Indeed, Canada possesses enormous resources of coal, large deposits of low-grade iron ores, and almost certainly a great potential wealth in oil. In nickel, asbestos, cobalt, gold, silver, copper, lead and zinc, the Dominion has been or is likely to become one of the largest exporters in the world. And equally in the output of chromite, feldspar, graphite, gypsum, mica, magnesite,

84

pyrites, and talc Canada has a yield and a promise which hardly any country in the world can rival. A significant evidence of the importance of the mining industry is to be found in the fact that to that industry belongs over thirty-five per cent. of the tonnage carried by Canadian railways.

Another source of Canadian wealth little understood abroad, and perhaps imperfectly appreciated even at home, is to be found in her commercial fisheries. Two of the great sea-fishing areas of the world border on Canada. And even more surprising—the lakes and rivers of the Dominion constitute almost one-half of the fresh water of the globe. The Atlantic coast line from Labrador to the boundary between the United States and Canada measures over five thousand miles. It includes the Bay of Fundy, eight thousand square miles in area, the Gulf of St. Lawrence, nearly eighty thousand square miles, and other waters which make the total area almost exactly two hundred thousand square miles. On the far side of the continent, the Pacific coast line is over seven thousand miles long, and the fresh-water lakes of the interior flow over an area of two hundred and twenty thousand square miles. The share of Canada in the Great Lakes along the United States boundary amounts to thirty-four thousand square miles.

The total annual yield of edible fishes of all kinds, which in 1918 (I have no later return) reached the record sum of seven hundred and sixty million, leaves Canada third among the fishing countries of the world, Great Britain still being first, and the United States second.

The resources of this impressive country are therefore as immense as they are manifold. Patience and imagination must indeed march hand in hand in order to develop the bountiful inheritance which at present is in the hands of so few.

But of the superb future—ultimately as

stupendous as that of the United States—there is no doubt. And the facts upon which this prediction is cautiously founded should be known to every Englishman.

I noticed much development in the field of manufacture. And here was observable a curious side light upon the effect of the British tariff upon motor cars. This duty admitted of reduction in favour of Dominion exporters. American manufacturers, feeling the pinch of the tax and anxious to obtain the advantage of the Canadian reduction, have established numerous large automobile factories in the Dominion, employing thousands of Canadian workmen and making no small contribution to Canadian rates and taxes.

A considerable—if less dependable—source of revenue in the Dominion at this moment has its origin in that system of Prohibition in the United States which I have already analysed in a separate chapter. It is plainly impossible to prevent smuggling over a boundary thousands of miles long. To do it effectively would require the employment of almost the whole adult male population of the United States. It is unquestionable that, directly and indirectly, the American sumptuary law has brought enormous sums into the Dominion. It need not be insisted how profitable is the mere business of smuggling which proceeds all the time, by road and lake, by day and night, with such general impunity as to suggest the existence of a friendly sympathy on each side of the boundary line. But smuggling does not exhaust the matter. Very great benefits to Canadian holiday and pleasure resorts in town and country alike have resulted from the contrast between the social laws of the two countries. The number of travellers, for instance, in the Far West, in the Rocky Mountains, and other picturesque touring grounds, has undergone great increase; while in Montreal the swift erection of a third enormous hotel is to be ex-plained in some small measure by the swelling numbers of American visitors.

The present population of Canada is nine millions. One sometimes hears impatient criticism of the comparative slowness with which, as it is supposed, that total grows. And yet, if one selects a relative and comparable period in the history of the United States, it will be found that the growth of the Dominion has rivalled in swiftness that of her gigantic neighbour. And the signs of a swift and marvellous expansion are everywhere observable. There is first the rude clearing; then a pathetic and rudimentary "Main Street," with perhaps a tiny church and a versatile store. Return in two to three years, and you find that there is already developed a small and prosperous townlet.

I often recalled, as I took note of development since my last visit, the eloquent words of Burke when an earlier empire was at the hazard:

Whether I put the numbers too high or too low is a matter of little moment. Such is the strength with which the population shoots in that part of the world that, set the numbers as high as we will, whilst the dispute continues, the exaggeration ends. Whilst we are discussing any given magnitude, they are grown to it. Whilst we spend our time in deliberating on the mode of governing 2,000,000 we shall find we have more millions to manage. Your children do not grow faster from infancy to manhood than they spread from families to communities, and from villages to nations.

It is, however, unquestionably true that a more rapid development of her numbers would bring to the Dominion a swift and very great accession of prosperity and wealth. The population is only nine millions: the national equipment would almost carry twenty. Nor are the housing difficulties which would be occasioned by a great increase comparable to those which beset an older civilisation. For in spite of reckless fire wastage, the forest resources of Canada are still incalculably great; and the standard houses of the countryside, as also in the poorer districts of the cities, are invariably wood. This kind of house seems to me to present many advantages. It is durable. It is warm. It is capable of swift erection; and as some of the exquisite New England architecture remains to teach us, it admits of a quaint and picturesque beauty of its own. I have indeed often wondered that Dr. Addison did not substitute an experiment in wood for some of his own less satisfactory conceptions. The housing problem, then, will not arise in any serious form; the great problem, therefore, before the Dominion statesmen is to attract to their country in sufficient numbers settlers of the right kind. It ought not to exhaust their contrivance and ours to correlate the difficulties of these islands, which spring in no small measure from overpopulation, with those of the Dominion, many of which arise conversely from underpopulation. These matters were made the subject of much discussion at the

recent Colonial Conference, and might with
advantage be examined again by the leaders
of the Socialist Party, who have hitherto
brought little enlightenment to the subject
of emigration. One thing is essential. A
strong central committee of British and
Canadian experts, with branches both at
home and in the Dominion, must make it
their business to see that the right kind of
emigrant is sent to the right kind of place.
The most pressing need, of course, is for
trained agricultural labourers; but for
capable artisans, properly advised, the
means of a comfortable subsistence is assured. The benefits which would follow a
great increase in the British elements of the
population are obvious and manifold. Of
the political side I will speak later; but it is
evident upon a purely business consideration that the development of the population and resources of the Dominion would
very greatly increase the Canadian market for British products, so that our prob-

lems of congestion would find relief at both ends.

I found in the country a certain amount of anxiety caused by the great recent increases in the American tariff. For evident reasons Canada neither hopes nor aspires to establish a very effective competition in manufactured goods upon the other side of the frontier. But there are many staple articles which she could and gladly would export if the tariff afforded her any reasonable prospect of penetrating into the American market. In the main it does not do so, and the realisation is now general that the United States have hardened into an unshakable conviction, based upon principle, that a rigid system of protection is consonant with, and even required by, the national interest. Business opinion in the Dominion is fully alive to this circumstance, and there is, I think, a general desire to examine with sympathy all reasoned proposals which aim at increasing the general

total of inter-imperial trade. In this connection the additional preference proposals,
which those present at the last Imperial
Conference undertook to recommend to their
various constituents, excited a warm interest in Canada. While I am satisfied that the
withdrawal of these proposals, following
upon the change of government, would produce a disappointment equally keen, I cannot detect any tendency to make really bitter
complaint if any single parliament declined
to ratify these proposals; and while I found
everywhere a mild surprise at what Cana-
dians in their hearts consider the tenacious
pedantry of our adherence to a one-sided
system of free imports, I found equally a
complete recognition that the selection of
the economic system which suits us best is
a matter which British statesmen are bound
to consider in exclusive reference to British
interests as they see them. But side by side
with this recognition, and a little qualifying
its completeness, exists the view, widely

held, though always of course courteously expressed, that British interests must be interpreted with a larger rather than a parochial vision. The dream of an Empire almost self-supporting, because it produces in one territory or another almost everything which human existence and even human luxury requires; of an Empire wherein the component elements retain each and all (for this is elementary) their fiscal independence, but in which each and all are prepared to make some concessions to other members of the family for the Imperial conception: this dream, I am sure, has influenced and will continue to influence the ablest business men and statesmen in Canada. How far its realisation has been permanently affected by the recent unhappy election in this country it is not at the moment possible to predict. But it has been greatly compromised and certainly postponed. A general tariff without which really effective mutual preferences are not practicable has been hissed off the stage, not indeed because the play was a bad one, but because some of the performers did not know their parts; and because the audience had come to the theatre on a too sudden invitation, not knowing what the play was about. In the result the only great party which really believed in Protection has been driven—it had no choice—to remove this cause from its proximate programme. The formula now is that the reform is incapable of attainment except as the fruit of an almost general agreement. The prospect may well strike our friends in Canada and Australia as gloomy. It is, however, when all the necessary admissions are made, less gloomy than it sounds. For just as the Conservative Party is the only party which believes in Protection as a faith, so the Liberal Party, here as always out of date, is the only party which believes in Free Trade as a faith. The Socialist Party is not only upon this subject open to conviction. It is bound to be convinced. Every consideration of logic, every compulsion of consistency, must lead them in the wide field of international economics to pursue the road which and which alone in domestic matters has supplied them with a thread of homogeneous principle. And when that moment comes at last, the dwindling forces of Liberalism (if indeed any still survive) will be found still mumbling incantations before a dead effigy in an abandoned shrine.

In this connection it is worth analysing very briefly the imports into Canada from the United Kingdom during some of the years from 1897 to 1922. It will be remembered that the British preference was approved by the Canadian Government on the 1st of August, 1898, and did not become completely effective until during the year 1899. In 1897, the total imports under consideration amounted to $29,000,000 (for simplicity I give the figures in terms of millions), of which $9,000,000 was free. In

1900 the total increased to $44,000,000, of which $12,000,000 was free; in 1910, $95,-000,000, of which $23,000,000 was free; in 1920 the total was $126,000,000, of which $33,000,000 was free. The total for 1921 was, however, remarkable, amounting as it did to imports of the total value of $213,-000,000, of which $40,000,000 was free. The corresponding figures for the year 1922 were: total imports, $117,000,000; free imports, $21,000,000. In the last ten years the rough average of the total imports has been $115,000,000 and the rough average of the free imports $28,000,000.

These figures speak for themselves and make it plain how enormous is the present value of the existing Canadian preference to the workingmen of this country; and, even more conspicuously, how great is the total value to these islands of the whole Canadian trade. The moral which ought to be drawn from these remarkable figures is surely plain enough. Everywhere in Europe we see stagnation, uncertainty and decay. Nowhere else in the world, except in our own Dominions, can we hope to find markets in substitution for those which we have lost, either permanently or for a long time, as a result of the War. While it is not claimed that in any proximate period of time Empire markets, old or new, can fully supply all that we have lost, it is claimed, and indeed it is certain, that with sagacious statesmanship the existing markets within the Empire can be enormously increased. Unhappily, now that we have reverted in Great Britain to that form of single-party Government which so many short-sighted people acclaimed, we have released against the necessary proposal to grant the Dominions reciprocal preference a volume of factious hostility as dishonest as it is bitter. And so it happens to-day that there is almost a general, if a despairing recognition among Tariff Reformers in Great Britain that until the inexorable logic of our economic situation, present and future, has taught its harsh lessons, our own indispensable contribution to reciprocal preference cannot be carried through by the efforts of a single party, however devoted.

### The Imperial Connection, and the Position of Canada in the Empire.

This subject, always delicate, cannot be considered altogether apart from some of the matters which have been examined in the earlier part of this chapter. For it is now generally realised by sensible people that the coincidence of sentimental and material interest is stronger for Imperial purposes than either sentimental interest alone or material interest alone. And therefore every consideration of Imperial patriotism should incline those citizens of the Empire, wherever they live, who desire to maintain them, most zealously to exclude from their minds all pedantry and prejudice which might impede the attempt to increase the range of business accommodation between the component parts and the Mother Country. There are to be found, unquestionably, throughout the Dominion, innumerable citizens of British extraction who need no stimulus to their devotion. Some of these are the descendants of those loyal Americans who sought a new home under the British Flag rather than acquiesce in the issue of the American revolt. Others have emigrated in their own lifetimes. Indeed, in this connection it is of interest to notice that of those who fought in the first gallant Canadian Division, of whom so many perished in the Second Battle of Ypres, the majority were actually born in Great Britain. Others, again, belong to families whose fathers or grandfathers were the first emigrants; and many of these have refreshed their knowledge of England by frequent visits. Canadian citizens of this kind are uninfluenced, or almost uninfluenced, by the business and political difficulties to

101

which I have made brief allusion. But it should never be forgotten that the origins of Canadian immigration have been much modified in recent years. In the Far West a great number of American farmers have crossed the border and exchanged their nationality. While we may expect from these an attitude of reasonable friendliness, it would be absurd to look for any special sympathy with British institutions or a very general conception of the meaning of Empire. The same observation applies with much greater force to that Scandinavian infusion which has been a noticeable element among immigrants in the last fifteen years. Many of these, naturally enough, see not the slightest reason for maintaining any connection at all with some small islands four thousand miles away. Indeed, the great majority living inland have hardly given a thought to the existence or the work of the British Navy. It is evident, therefore, that in a population diverse in its national origins and sparsely scattered over a gigantic continent, dogmatic generalisations are extremely unsafe. We may, however, for our encouragement, take notice that on three great and critical occasions there has been elicited from the Canadian people a spontaneous expression of affection and loyalty which no Englishman can recall without profound emotion.

The first of these was excited by the outbreak of the South African War. Here the resolute determination of the people themselves forced upon the Government, which at that moment believed action to be premature, the recognition that Canada must play some effective part in the field. And so it happened, by a dramatic chance, that the very turning point of that struggle was marked by the decisive valour of Canadian soldiers; for the troops of the Dominion played the principal part in storming at the point of the bayonet the laager behind which sullen Kronje lay at bay.

The second of these occasions arose when the Canadian Government of the day attempted to negotiate a general commercial treaty with the United States of America. In the course of the discussions an American Senator incautiously and in a public speech advocated the absorption of the Dominion at the hands of the United States. From that moment the suggested treaty was doomed, and the resultant election showed that, friendly as the relations between these two great countries were and are, the citizens of the Dominion are inflexibly determined to maintain their existing status.

Of the third I need hardly speak, for it is still fresh in our minds. The part played by the Dominion in the Great War will never fade from the memories of Englishmen, and has added a new and brilliant page to the long records of our martial achievements. Canada proved—what the prejudices of our regular army never gave our amateur soldiers the chance of proving—

that it is not only possible to improvise troops equal to the best conscript armies in the world, but that it is also possible to improvise generals who certainly need not fear comparison with those of the regular Army.

The material contribution made by the Dominion to the fortunes of the War were stupendous; but even that effort was hardly more important than the glowing moral influence which her adoption of all that underlay the struggle brought to our exertions. Homer once wrote of brothers:

"Those upon whom a man relies even though a great struggle arises."

To the daughter states within the Empire, as we throw our minds back to this titanic and often uncertain struggle, we may apply and adapt this noble family attribute.

It may perhaps be added that more Englishmen of position ought to realise the usefulness of visiting Canada in order to learn at first hand the resources of this wonderful country and the kindliness of this adventurous people. Nor will they be wise to confine their visits to the well-known cities of the East. No man knows Canada who has not made the journey to Vancouver—soon perhaps to be the greatest of Canadian cities—and Victoria. From such visits nothing but good can come. There will follow better acquaintance, and better acquaintance operating upon common history and traditions will deepen into vivid affection, so that as the rolling seasons pass, we shall witness the ties between the Islands and this mighty country ever deepening in sympathy and in intensity.

# CHAPTER IV

## PROBLEMS LEFT BY THE GREAT WAR

(Address by the Earl of Birkenhead, former Lord Chancellor of Great Britain, at the closing session of the Institute of Politics, Williamstown, Massachusetts, Friday evening, August 24, 1923.)

MR. PRESIDENT, LADIES AND GENTLEMEN: I count myself fortunate that I should have been invited by your distinguished president to take part, however late in the day, in the yearly work of that Institute of Politics which was the result, I believe, almost entirely of his own inspiration, and which has brought so much distinction not only in this country but in Europe to the ancient college with which that course will always be associated.

It is, I think, indisputable that the present mischiefs in the world can only reach—

if they can in any way reach—a solution
by discussion and debate. For without discussion and debate action not only cannot
be helpful, it may be positively injurious;
and the methods by which, as I conceive
them, conscientious, laborious, and sustained
discussions are carried on here seem to me
to reproduce in a modern age somewhat the
atmosphere in which in ancient days the
Socratic dialogues were inspired.

Now I propose, if I may, to indicate to
you at the outset the method which I may
most helpfully pursue, if indeed it is in my
power at all to give you any assistance in
relation to the topic which I had chosen. I
am conscious that everything that is ideal
must have been dealt with probably far more
fruitfully at the hands of the extremely competent and experienced experts who have
been debating these topics for, I believe, no
less a period than a month. And I may be
allowed to say that it would not be creditable
either to their originality or to their indus-

try if they had not in a month produced far more sound and instructive wisdom than can possibly be in my power to reproduce in an hour, even if I had enjoyed the benefits, which I have not, of listening to their discussions or of reading them.

I propose, therefore, with your good will, to attempt in the first place a short series of generalisations upon the subject which I have chosen, the subject, namely: Problems Left by the Great War. After I have attempted that short series of generalisations I shall ask your attention, not, I hope, for too long a period, to some more particular observations which I shall ask leave to make upon some of those problems which seem to me to be the gravest and the most difficult. I am well aware that the subject which I have chosen must involve me in a controversy. Indeed, I am told that even in the harmonious and quiet and charming atmosphere of this town you have not been able at times entirely to expel the controversial element from the discussions which have preceded my entry into this arena.

While, therefore, I must treat certain matters in a way which is not only controversial, but perhaps acutely controversial, and with an appearance of dogmatism which can never be avoided when curtailment is imperatively required by the occasion—while, I say, I shall try as far as possible to avoid either an unduly partial statement of that which I hope to indicate, or an unduly dogmatic method of presenting it, I am conscious that no human ingenuity could avoid this double risk.

I will, if you will permit me, make a few observations first as to an earlier stage of the problem which to-night demands our attention; for, though the stage is earlier, the problem is the same.

The circumstances amid which the Great War arose were astonishing enough. About twelve very unscrupulous but very powerful men decided, sitting around a table, that there should be war. They deliberated very privately in Berlin. Many cool observers in the world had doubted whether there would be war. I did not happen to be among the number. But there was much to be said for their view; in fact, there was almost everything to be said for it; for no one charged with the destinies of Germany could pronounce for war unless, besides being an extremely unprincipled, he was also an extremely ignorant, man. For Germany, given peace, had everything in her own hands, and her principal trade competitor in Europe was likely to be paralysed by internal dissensions relating to Ireland, which might easily have produced civil war. All Germany had to do was to wait. But, none the less, these twelve narrow, ignorant, arrogant men pronounced in favour of war. Their decisions psychologically had only to consider a weak monarch and a Crown Prince disloyal to that monarch. They triumphed, and from their triumph proceed the devastating consequences with which we and our children, and perhaps our children's children, must reckon for the rest of our and their lives.

The problems of the War were incalculably great; but they were small indeed compared with the problems of the peace. It took ten years to re-create the structure of European society after the Napoleonic wars; and the exhausting expenditure, material and vital, upon those wars was as nothing compared with that of which it is our duty to make a cool analysis.

It is no use abusing the Treaty of Versailles. That treaty was the creature of the victorious mood of the victorious allies. It is quite easy now to say that more moderate terms could and ought to have been imposed. The answer is complete. Human nature being what it is, no victorious nations could have reconciled with the determination of their democracies terms less severe upon a defeated enemy who had deliberately

112

and wickedly, for motives of national aggrandisement, run the risk of submerging the whole of Western civilisation. President Wilson, indeed, came with a noble message of hope; but, unhappily, in the sequel, hope proved to be his principal equipment. It is a fascinating speculation whether, had he been given health and strength to pursue the campaign which he contemplated, his idealism and personality could have affected the forces of the world. I am bold enough, even at the moment when I pay the highest tribute to his unselfish and courageous motives, to doubt it. For the real truth is that while the whole world requires the encouragement and the light of idealism, the whole world would probably not survive if idealism were given a completely free rein. The same simple, illuminating—if cynical— truth applies to that hideous competition in the world by which every individual who does not inherit a fortune is confronted. The great Bentham long since pointed out

113

that the motive spring, and the necessary motive spring, of human endeavour, was self-interest; and he equally pointed out that the consequences would certainly be obscure, and in his judgment would be unfortunate, if every individual began to regulate his or her life, not upon his or her own interests, but upon some supposed interest of others. And, indeed, a very cautious mind might stagger before such a possibility. No creature in the world—human, animal, or, it might also be added, vegetable—has ever regulated his, her, or its life upon a basis such as that under consideration. And when it is considered that the world has already lasted for some millions (or billions) of years, and that countless billions of breathing creatures have inhabited this world during that period, an experience so unanimous and so entirely unaffected, either by Christianity or by civilisation, at least affords to a scientific observer the material for an irresistible generalisation.

And the same great truth applies equally to nations. No nation in democratic conditions will ever be allowed to become the knight-errant of the world. The governors of each nation are the trustees of the whole people; and, unhappily, they are removable trustees. They must always keep pace with the beneficiaries of the trust because the beneficiaries in this particular matter can at any moment discharge them from their offices. And therefore, it seems to me that while the name of President Wilson must always be revered by those who render homage to purposes almost superhuman, pursued with a zeal almost as superhuman, yet it must none the less be recognised that his judgment of his own countrymen was wrong, and that by the error of that judgment he became, paradoxically enough, the agent of all those post-war developments from which his altruistic mind would most specially have recoiled.

I, for myself, have no delusions as to the

only function which the American Government is called upon to discharge. Their primary, and indeed their only duty, is to the American people. If by intervention in the affairs of a stricken Europe they can advance the fortunes of the American people, then it seems to me, as a humble observer, that it would be their duty to make such an intervention. But if in cool perspective they reached the conclusion that no compensating gain to the American people would result from reassuming European and world responsibility, they would be failing in their duty if they embraced an unnecessary responsibility.

This, and this alone, is the problem of the moment. Who shall marshal the arguments? The most acute and learned political dialectician in the world might fly from the task in despair. And, indeed, the great economists and financiers of the world have in the last four years proved little able to afford us sound guidance or even accurate prediction. Who is there to-day who has appreciated the complete economic consequences of the accumulation of so much gold in America upon the export trade of America? Who is there who can tell us clearly over how long a period the immense domestic market of the United States will be adequate for the equally immense manufacturing resources of your great cities? Who has yet convincingly analysed, in relation to the devastating problems of modern ex.hanges, the effect of a high-tariff system? Who has accurately measured the effect upon the agricultural community of the United States of the existing and artificially produced economic conditions? The farmers of the Middle West have long, in my understanding of American history, been among the great figures of your ordered community. They have been efficient; they have been industrious; they have been conservative in the sense of being non-political, an adjective in which all reasonable men see praise. Are the present conditions of the world favourable, or even tolerable, to them? Are they likely to improve? Are they affected by the present condition of the world? Can their condition be permanently alleviated while the conditions of that stricken world remain unchanged? If I am right in supposing that the deflated condition of Europe as Europe is to-day already affords grave anxiety to your agricultural community and may, in the future however remote, occasion an equal and analogous anxiety to your manufacturing community, I have at least established all that I care to establish: that grave and not very remote problems await the decision of the American nation.

For myself, I have never varied in my view. Great nations not only deserve, but require, a great world in which to develop their own greatness. Commercial genius flourishes when the whole world flourishes; and its prospects decline when the whole world declines. Shipping, invisible exchanges, interest on money borrowed by stable creditors—these are the garnered rewards afforded to the thrift and financial efficiency of the nations which are happy enough to possess those assets. But if you substitute for the conditions which existed before the War a world in which there are no markets for anything which you or we can produce, because hardly any one in the world can afford to buy at the present rate of exchanges that which you and we—both manufacturing nations—can produce, then, sooner or later, your experience must be the same as ours. The manufacturing genius of your nation is great; so is the manufacturing genius of ours. To-day we are suffering more than you in our manufacturing, if not in our agricultural community, because our home market is smaller than yours. But if and when your home market ceases to employ in their fullest energy the resources of your manufacturers, the resul-

119

tant position, combined with the existing agricultural situation, will bring you almost precisely to the position which to-day we feel. Nor will gold reserves help you. Nor have they very much helped any people in the world. The strength of the world lies neither in gold nor in precious jewels; it lies in the ordered and peaceful industry of great populations harnessed to those occupations by which, in the imperfectly defined purposes of the Author of the universe, all alike must earn their living. And the genius of great peoples, while we maintain our present economic systems, will find its reward in extricating a world of suffering, not unwilling to work, from its present morass, and in releasing and reanimating the economic forces which, and which alone, can bring prosperity to the body politic and economic of the whole world.

I indicated that I should precede the more particular observations I have to make by a series of generalisations which because they must necessarily be brief must equally necessarily be bold, and it has occurred to me that it might interest you if by way of some particular illustrations I indicated a few general conclusions as to the situation of several of the most important nations in Europe at this moment. And at least I make this claim with boldness, that if I err, if I do too much justice to one country and too little justice to another, it is not because I am not making a sincere and an honest attempt to see the situation as the situation actually is, excluding so far as I can exclude all national, all emotional, and all cosmopolitan prejudice from my mind. Let me, then, so far indulge the egotism of an Englishman by selecting first for consideration the case of my own country.

The generous admission of the American nation has been freely and generously made that England made sacrifices in the Great War, which I am content to be moderately stated in the words of a great American, that they were sacrifices worthy of the martial history of that country. I need not recall to you the loss of life almost comparable to that sustained by France, which has destroyed for ever the hopes of so many English homes with an anguish far more widely spread than that with which the Angel of Death enters alike the palace of the great and the home of the humble in your country. Still less do I speak insistently to-night of the treasure, collected painfully and industriously over centuries, which we flung without a thought and without a question into the common cause.

But I would ask your attention to the situation in England as we see that situation to-day. We have balanced our budget. We have not shrunk from a sustained stringency of taxation, comparable, to say the least, to that by which you yourselves are crushed at this moment. For that reason, our credit is high; we have followed—I know not whether we have followed too closely—the hard and painful road to deflation, rather than the easy primrose path to inflation; and by an incorrigible habit which our country has pursued through the centuries, which I think has not, perhaps, been without some resultant and compensating advantages to our credit in the world—we have an incorrigible habit of paying our debts. And this we have hitherto done whether we borrowed the money for our own consumption or for the accommodation of a friend who at that moment was in a difficulty. But such is our situation until I come to make a very brief observation on the subject of reparations. If I were right—at any rate, the great majority of the victorious nations will agree that I am right—in making the claim that this War with all its staggering cost in blood and treasure was forced by a guilty country upon a reluctant world—if that claim be not too bold, it follows plainly and unarguably from it that quite apart from the financial aspect of compensating those who were the innocent victims of an aggressive war and who sustained ruinous and devastating consequences in their financial affairs—it follows that quite apart from that consideration, for the mere warning of nations in the future, the price paid is and must be heavy.

But here, unhappily, the position of Great Britain is not especially favourable, because to us it sometimes seems as if almost all the world except ourselves lived in a universe of which the general atmosphere issued from a series of very astonishing illusions. It has sometimes seemed to us that there is a general view, certainly held almost universally in Europe, a general view that such is the simplicity of the British character, that this nation can be relied upon not merely to adopt a course, so far unimitated by others, of paying our just debts, but that we are also to forgive every one else, whoever they may be, everything that they may owe us, whatever the cause of that indebtedness is. Such an assumption, however gratifying to the

124

reputation which our country has established in history, however eloquent of the practical application which, almost alone among the nations, we are supposed to be capable of making and to have made—I say, however gratifying these tributes are, there are, I assure you, quite a considerable number of persons in England who are not able to subscribe to them.

For let me indicate to you by way of sample illustration what the consequences would be. But first of all let me give you, as I can do in one or two simple sentences, the general continental atmosphere to-day.

First of all, it is always assumed in Germany that "we shall have to pay something to France; we shall have to pay something to Belgium; we may have to pay something to Italy, but Great Britain, as a general accommodation, it may surely be assumed that Great Britain will waive her claim." Well, whether there will be much to waive as the centre part of Europe develops might be made a subject of curious controversy, and I do not pursue it now; but I rather pass to another source from which we might hope to obtain something; that is to say, from those allies who have taken the somewhat different view of sound finance to ourselves in the last four years and on whose behalf we guaranteed indebtedness during the years of the war. Their view of the matter seems to me to be an extremely simple one. It is quite true in a pedantic business sense you may say we owe this money to you, but pedantry is one thing and sentiment and realities are quite different things, and you really cannot ask us to pay you. I assure you that is the general atmosphere that is adopted in Europe. Suppose that we yield to it, tempted by the additional attraction offered, that if and when Germany pays a sum of money which everybody who is not in a lunatic asylum knows Germany can never pay,—"if and when she pays us in full, then we shall be delighted to pay you what we owe you." I myself should have been a much richer man if I had been able to regulate my own small matters of indebtedness upon a somewhat similar basis. In fact, only the other day I observed that an eloquent and well-known writer in a French paper said quite plainly, "Our debts—our debts—our debts are the scars of the war." That, of course, is one way of looking at the matter. I rather wish it had occurred to us. We looked at a debt of honour through different eyes.

Another writer, this time an Italian writer, in an article which was brought to my attention ten days ago, made the following illuminating observation. He said, "We are told that Great Britain is going to forgive us our debt to her." Who told him, I do not know. "Well, a year ago, we should have welcomed the assurance, but now it has been so generally acted upon that it ceases to cause us any particular excitement."

Observe, then, where my unfortunate

country is. We are not apparently to receive anything from the German reparations. We are not able to draw any considerable cheques upon that bank in which is kept an account for the scars of war. We are going, as it is our wish, and was always our fixed intention, for the reasons I have given, historical and inherent in the character of our people, to pay our own debts. We have not laid and do not propose to lay any complaint whatever, but in what situation will that leave us? If these gloomy apprehensions are acquiesced in they will leave us in this condition: that we, who, after all, were not more conspicuously defeated than another nation, are the only nation that is really paying indemnity, unless Germany pays some. This is perhaps a surprising result of the rather remarkable efforts we made during those four years. But if this be the result, it must be the result.

Such is the train of thought which is passing through many British minds. Let us see whether or not I can apply my judgment with equal impartiality to what I conceive to be the French view. For many years before the War France was bullied and humiliated by Germany in the face of the whole world. Instead of resting content with the striking victory which ended with the transfer to Germany of the province of Alsace-Lorraine, without being content with that, the bungling diplomacy of Germany, foolishly apprehensive of a swift expansion of Russian strength, neglected no occasion by which it might remind France that she had been a defeated, and in the judgment of Germany, was still a negligible nation. The legacy of bitterness and resentment which had been left by the campaign of Sedan deepened and intensified as the result of a brutal and insensate diplomacy. And so you came to this War—a war which incontestably, so far at least as we are concerned, we no longer propose to reargue, was forced by Germany upon France. A considerable part of France was devastated; inconceivable savageries were perpetrated in obedience to the doctrine of so-called horribleness. And at the end France undoubtedly feels, and in many ways France quite rightly feels, that Germany has not paid what Germany could pay, and that a deliberate attempt is being made by subterranean manipulations of the paper currency at home and by the export of assets abroad, to produce a bankruptcy which may indeed be official, but which has no correspondence with the actual and potential resources of the people measured in their material possessions and their organising power.

Such is the French conception, and there is, of course, much to be said for it. There is a great deal to be said for the view that you should obtain the maximum amount which is payable by Germany so long as you do not impair her capacity to pay anything at all.

I was myself opposed to the French occupation of the Ruhr, because neither you nor we have anything to gain by any further complications in the political situation in those districts. The only interest that we have in that situation—and you still retain some small financial interest—the only interest is whether or not the step which she is taking is one which is likely to produce a larger reparation; otherwise the matter does not concern us, except in its purely political side.

The French, however, went into the Ruhr, and the moment they went in I have always quite plainly maintained that they were committed and that the flag of France was committed to the experiment. And I see myself no means whatever, which are within our power to adopt or which it would be conceivable that we should adopt, to terminate that experiment. We may agree or we may disagree, but the French are in the Ruhr, and it is by the development of the situation which has been produced by their occupation, and by that development alone, that it will be shown whether they were right or whether we were. But we may be allowed solemnly to notice that whatever other compensating advantages—if there be compensating advantages—have flowed from the occupation of the Ruhr, the prospect of Great Britain obtaining any reparations at all has evidently been diminished.

I will now, if you would allow me, make a concluding observation upon the subject of Germany. I have not hesitated to state quite plainly my conception of the primary responsibility for the terrible War, the memories of which still, in their poignancy, throng our minds. But, while I make that observation there are certain circumstances which require to be borne in mind. It is necessary, for the correction and the warning of those who may be tempted in the future along the promising road of international crime—it is necessary to remind them that a nation cannot escape responsi-

132

bility and cannot evade punishment by pointing to its government and saying that they and not the nation are responsible. If such a plea were ever admitted the jurisprudence of a nation and the decisions of war would prove to be equally nugatory. Such a claim cannot be admitted, but a distinction must of course be drawn between the case of a democracy and that of a nation which lived under an autocracy, which had no real voice in its own government, which was powerless without a revolution to control the foreign policy of that government, and which found itself with easy promises of swift immediate material aggrandisement launched upon the primrose road which it had trod itself in previous historic campaigns. A distinction, I think, in justice must in this respect be drawn between a democracy which has deliberately maintained and supported a policy, and a nation upon which, under an autocrat or a military caste, that policy has been imposed. The distinction must not be

133

exaggerated nor its consequences magnified, but that there is such a distinction I do not doubt. And equally I do not doubt that there are many in Germany to-day, honest men, particularly of the middle classes, who have seen every farthing which they possessed dissipated while the mark joins the rouble in its devil's dance; men who had no more responsibility for the War than you and I had. I can conceive of many such thinking that there are respects in which they have not perhaps been afforded a real chance of making pecuniary reparation without involving themselves in complete ruin.

The first ground, therefore, upon which, if I were a German standing before you to-night, I should base a plea, not indeed for reconsideration of the major decisions, for those decisions are irrevocably taken, but at least for some degree of consideration and perhaps of reconsideration, would be thus: You must tell a people if you are going to involve them in the payment of immense sums of money, you must tell them not a fanciful figure which you state for the purposes of the impossible maximum, but you must tell them in real terms which you intend and are able to enforce, the amount which they must pay; and it must be an amount which conceivably at least they can pay. And therefore, I for one, and I think all English people, warmly welcome a proposal, of which I believe Secretary Hughes was the author, that a commission should be appointed in order to determine the amount which Germany can pay. But the unfortunate part of that suggestion, at the moment when it has been pressed for the adoption of the French nation, is that it has come when they are committed to the Ruhr experiment, and when in consequence they are almost logically committed to maintaining the authority of the Reparations Commission whose principal and primary function is to solve this very question, namely:

what Germany can pay.

I have tried to keep myself in the case of England in the position of an Englishman, not anxious to be partial or unfair, and to state the world situation as it strikes and must strike him. We know only too well that the direct consequence of the condition of Europe is the unemployment which has grown and grown in all our great cities and which seems likely to reach even a more sombre climax in the approaching autumn. Such, I think, would be the general view of the ordinary Englishman trying to state the position fairly and clearly.

I have tried to put myself in the position of a French citizen standing here and charged with the same duty before this great meeting. I hope that the points upon which I made it plain, that I found myself unable to agree with the policy of the French Government, have not made it impossible for me to appreciate the feelings which have operated in their minds or the bitterness and re-

sentment which have led them to so many
conclusions.

And, observe that it is equally our duty to
ascertain what points there are, if there be
any such points, which can be fairly placed
before a reasonable conqueror by a nation
which has been defeated. I cannot eliminate
from my mind any more than you can eliminate from yours the uneasy activities of
various great financial figures in Germany
who have been enabled by transfers of capital and by the conversion of paper into solid
and more durable assets, to produce some
of the amazing consequences which have recently marked the downward fall of German currency. I cannot say whether the
situation and these charges, for they are
openly made, are ill founded, but I should
not exhaust the possibilities which are entertained as to the actual situation in Germany
if I did not remind you that by a well-
informed section of European opinion these
views are commonly held.

That which I had to say to you is concluded. Who can doubt that I use moderate language when I say that the War has bequeathed to Europe perplexing and it may be ruinous problems? Great Britain cannot indefinitely support the burden of unemployment which has involved us, and necessarily, in my opinion, involved us, in the payment over so many years of such gigantic sums. To us it is necessary, for we are neither self-supporting nor primarily agricultural; to us it is necessary that we should replace the markets that we have lost or cease to maintain an industrial population upon our soil.

The gravity and difficulty of this problem have not been diminished by the circumstances that our population has grown on a scale so surprising as it has done since the War. France has her problems. Germany, of all others, has her own. Is there any ray of hope which at this moment can be presented? Can any alleviation be found,

I neither claim nor ask nor hope in the near future, but in a period of five or even ten years? I should not deal honestly with you if I concealed from you my own conclusion, that unless some change unforeseen by me, unforeseeable by me, occurs in the present situation, the condition of all Europe must grow progressively worse.

We can indeed, no doubt, modelling ourselves upon your exceptional geographical situation and resources, more and more deflect British credits into our own dominions and extend and encourage our colonial markets. We can more and more reassert the British policy of isolation sustained for so many centuries teeming with great historic events. We can say to Europe, "Continue if you will the ruinous courses to which you are committed, the British Empire will appeal to its own people, will develop its own markets, will concentrate its finances and its own resources upon its own dominion." And yet, this is a part which I should myself be sorry to see carried to its sad and cynical conclusion. A tragic moment comes when nations who trod together so many years the bloody road of death, who breathed so many years the black air almost of despair, say at the one moment when the battle has been won after so much struggle and so much endeavour, "We carried through that incredible and man-destroying task; from the minor task of statecraft that remained we have recoiled in mutual estrangement."

I still hope and I still believe, though I am not bold enough to express this feeling in terms of time—I still hope and I still believe that all the nations who saved civilisation, which would otherwise have been destroyed, will one day realise and convince themselves that they rightly realise that not merely the interest of Europe but the individual interest of every great country in the world requires that some common effort shall be made to alleviate and correct the misery under which Europe is groaning to-day and before which Europe may so easily succumb. Then, not only shall be won the greatest war in history but our names will be remembered and acclaimed by generations to come as the men who were not unequal to a nobler task, that of winning the greatest peace in history.

# CHAPTER V

IT would have appeared to me a little egotistical that I should use your invitation to address the American Bar Association by attempting a disquisition upon the British constitution and its developments in half a century. But I was assured by a very distinguished American legal authority that the subject would be neither disagreeable nor unattractive to American lawyers, and it was pointed out to me that if the matter were examined from a converse angle, the writings of the late Lord Bryce upon the Constitution of the United States of America had never failed to excite the interest and the admiration of British lawyers, and I may equally add that the recent lectures

142

upon your Supreme Court delivered at Gray's Inn in London excited a wide degree of professional interest.

And perhaps the subject matter of these few observations may be defended upon a broader ground. No service is rendered to Anglo-American relations by exaggerating the debt which you owe either to our Constitution or to our jurisprudence. But nevertheless that debt is very great. In constitutional matters the peculiar genius of American statesmen has produced a complex system in which much to an Englishman seems wholly admirable and much, if he be permitted the criticism, of more disputable value.

One thing at least is certain. The framers of the American Constitution produced something which was original and which purchased certain acknowledged advantages at the cost of certain hardly disputable disadvantages. But your forbears chose their own course. They were strong men, seeing as far as most men of their day and generation could see.

Whether if some divine revelation had forewarned them of the incredible development in the values of world importance which awaited your nation they would still have formulated your primary constitutional document in the same terms I cannot tell. I suspect that while they might have reasoned with such knowledge that the prospect savoured of megalomania they would still have pursued the same policy. They would perhaps have said:

> We do not ask to see the distant scene,
> One step enough for us.

And herein they would have been right. They were strong men with clear views. They were the pilots of an immediate and obscure voyage. Their evident and immediate responsibilities were contemporary.

These observations are not intended to suggest that the genius of the framers of

144

the American Constitution has not been
justified by the years that have supervened.
They are intended rather to make it plain,
without establishing comparative valuations, how profoundly their conceptions dif-
fered from the British conception of constitutional evolution. I suspect, without find-
ing leisure to discuss the matter here, that
the explanation is to be found in the contemporary political atmosphere.

But the difference between the two constitutions is profound. It may ultimately
prove to be a difference altogether creditable
to the genius of your forbears. The last
verdict upon this issue will not be pronounced until your industrial and social
questions, in which I am daring enough to
include your Negro problem, have reached
a longer and a more sophisticated test. It
may, for instance, well be that two centuries
more must pass before any man can be sure
of the future alignment and the future
strength of the Labour party in America.

Your problems at this moment are not comparable to ours, simply because the infusion of your population has proceeded from channels so cosmopolitan. Discordant languages and traditions do not lend themselves for generations to a homogeneous socialist creed—perhaps they will not do so for two hundred years.

The forces which as inevitably in your country as in any other must one day be challenged will not effect the cohesion by which an older European civilisation is to-day confronted. But one day that issue will be sharply challenged. And then and not until then will it be fully realised how far the barriers which the framers of your Constitution imposed upon the complete freedom of your legislative assemblies have been justified by the longer prevision.

Upon the Negro problem, upon the labour problem and their contingent anxieties it would ill become one who is not an American to make a rash intrusion. But any honest analyst of contemporary politics and of the effect of the element to which I have made a passing reference must recognise at once that this question cannot be permanently eliminated from an examination of the comparative merits of a constitution ultimately controlled by the judicature and of a constitution not so controlled.

For herein lies the fundamental difference between your Constitution and ours. Your Constitution is expressed and defined in documents which can be pronounced upon by the Supreme Court. In this sense your judges are the masters of your executive. Your Constitution is a cast-iron document. It fails to be construed by the Supreme Court with the same sense of easy and admitted mastery as any ordinary contract. This circumstance provides a breakwater of enormous value against ill-considered and revolutionary change.

Whether if the forces behind revolutionary change become menacing and strong

enough the breakwater will serve must be
left for the future to determine. But an
outsider must fully and absolutely admit
that up to the present its strength has
seemed extremely adequate.

Your President is one for whom intellectually I have a great admiration, and per-
sonally a deep affection. His masterly address to-day carried me entirely with him.
But surely one refinement was a little subtle.
He said that the Supreme Court had not the
right *in abstracto* to construe your fundamental constitutional document, but only in
relation to the issues presented by an individual litigation. But is this in ultimate
analysis a very serious derogation? When
an issue challenged by an individual raises
the question whether a law is constitutional
or not, the decision of the Supreme Court
decides this question for all time, or if the
decision is against the legislation the attempted law is stripped of its attempted
authority.

148

# AMERICAN BAR ADDRESS

In Great Britain, rightly or wrongly, we have proceeded upon a different basis from yours. The genius of the Anglo-Saxon people has, again rightly or wrongly, refused to shackle in the slightest degree the constitutional competence of later generations. And thus it happens that practically no law in Great Britain is constitutional in the sense in which you have a constitution. Any law in Great Britain can be altered by any Parliament and no court may challenge the constitutional force of any act of Parliament. The late Professor Dicey distinguished the two forms of constitution by calling one rigid and the other flexible. On the whole I prefer to call the one controlled and the other uncontrolled. The difference is prodigious whatever label you prefer. It is on the whole premature to decide whether you or we have been right.

But the ease with which the gravest political changes may be made in Great Britain has afforded and will afford anxiety in the future. For uncontrolled power and an imperfectly educated democracy go ill together. In England we have chosen to take these risks. In America you have, on the whole, chosen to avoid them. It is not uninstructive to observe the changes which have taken place in the constitution of Great Britain in the fifty or sixty years which have witnessed political readjustments so immense and far-reaching.

Sixty years ago Great Britain was the mother of representative and parliamentary institutions. But still she was not a democracy. The menacing fights associated with the great Reform Act were in contact with the issues of a graver day like the military minuets of eighteenth-century continental warfare.

There was neither reality nor vitality in the results. The formidable controversy which arose on the famous Reform Bill, which nearly brought down the House of Lords and might quite easily have involved the monarchy, increased the electorate but only by a despicable percentage which could not in any degree that mattered deflect the centre of political gravity. The increase of voters proposed was hardly more than that of three to five per cent. Wellington, Gladstone, Disraeli, all played their parts in a controversy which was largely unreal, because the changes proposed, and so bitterly disputed, were really so unimportant.

The genius of Disraeli, contemptuous of the taunt, not unjustly made against him, of inconsistency, made the first real change. And thereafter progressively the advance has proceeded. And in the furnace of the Great War, Great Britain took the immense responsibility of handing over to the masses of her population the control of her destinies though her legislators well knew that no written constitution and no law court could fetter or clog the completeness of that which was given.

Far the greatest development, therefore,

in the British constitution in the last sixty years is that which has handed over absolutely without reserve the control of the government of Great Britain. This charter so given will never, it may be confidently predicted, be withdrawn by law. If we give a rein to curious speculation we may wonder whether the powers so given if insanely exercised will be corrected by a movement so astonishing as the Fascisti movement in Italy. Short of this nothing could or would correct the uncontrolled power, which now lies at the disposal of the pencil of the British electorate.

First, then, of all of the great developments to be noted in the last sixty years is that which has swept aside the last vestige of real territorial influence over British politics and has left the whole of an ancient and glorious constitution in the melting pot to be moulded by unknown and incalculable forces. I shall be unwilling to be supposed an overanxious critic of these revolutions, anxious as they are. For I profoundly believe in the common sense and in the fundamental sanity of the Anglo-Saxon race. For if one did not so believe one could only despair. The numbers of those who have hardly anything of that which seriously counts is so much greater than the number of those who have, that if a crude campaign of class hatred had any prospect of real success in Great Britain it would be certain.

But while I acknowledge many causes for grave anxiety I am none the less of opinion that the fundamental sobriety and poise of the British people, even with full allowance for an untested electorate, will attain to a just perspective and pronounce honest decisions. And yet this question cannot be exhausted without examining another tendency very observable to-day in Great Britain which at first sight might appear to be rather concerned with politics or with sociology than with constitutional development. But such an impression would be superficial and even delusive. For nothing could more closely relate to the topic of constitutional development than the emergence of an immense political force whose claim one day to form a government can no longer be disputed, and whose expressed views, if they so succeed, must profoundly, and perhaps for all time, affect the workings of the British constitution.

Twenty-five years ago when Parliament met, one solitary pioneer of the Socialist movement was returned to the House. This was Mr. Keir Hardie. Though a rugged, he was, I think, a sincere, man; this at least is certain; he clearly discerned that the political future of labour lay in the complete divergence through both the older parties. He was in fact the founder of the Independent Labour Party. From this small beginning the movement has continuously grown. The following election brought to Mr. Hardie some twelve followers who drove amid a cheering mob into the palace yard, presage

154

to those who had eyes to see the beginnings of the most formidable development.

At the last general election one hundred and fifty members of this party were returned to the House so that it now exceeds the aggregate strength of the Liberals led by Mr. Asquith or those who recognise Mr. Lloyd George as their leader. In these circumstances the official of the opposition was chosen from the ranks of the Labour Party and it would follow in obedience to the covenants of our constitution that if the present government were defeated as the result of a Socialist attack in Parliament that the King would send for Mr. Ramsay MacDonald to form a government.

It is not my purpose here to discuss the results which would attend the attempt of the Socialist Party to carry the constituents in sufficient strength to make them the governors of Great Britain. I speak here as a lawyer among lawyers, quite dispassionately, measuring probabilities precisely as

I should measure them in order to base upon my conclusion decision and action.

And I am not on the whole of opinion that an early success awaits the Socialist Party in Great Britain. They are divided among themselves. They are honeycombed by rivalries and jealousies. They do not agree upon many fundamental principles. They cannot unite, unless it be in opposition. It would carry me far from my present purpose to examine the merits either of a capital levy or of the socialisation of the means of production, distribution and exchange.

It is sufficient for me to say that in my judgment whether these proposals be good or whether they be bad on their merits the immediate result of either will be so to deflate British credit through the world that the whole of that majestic edifice might easily crumble before a foundation proven to be unsound. And in my opinion, that sanity and sobriety of the British people, in which I have already expressed my complete confidence, would at the critical moment recoil from a risk so tremendous. I myself am of opinion that a labour government would not, if it were afforded an opportunity, prove to be altogether unconservative.

It would be very nervous. It would be very anxious to avoid the obvious criticism that it was destroying the foundations of commerce and industry. The principal enemy of labour success in Great Britain to-day is not, in my judgment, anything which a labour government would succeed in effecting. It is the apprehension in the minds of a majority of the electors and that which they might do if they held the reins of power. The relevance of this topic to my general theme to-night lies in the certain effect upon our constitution of Socialist success, if and when Socialism attains such a success.

In the first place the House of Lords would cease to be an efficient instrument of government. Its reform, too long delayed, would become imperative. And that reform would lie in the hands of men in sympathy with history, its traditions or its character. To begin with, no real Labour minister would be, and none could or would, in the existing circumstances, become a member of that House. The mere fact that there is a possibility, which no cautious politician can altogether disregard, that the Labour Party may at some period, not altogether remote, be returned to power, would appear to make it imperative upon those who are in office to-day that they should effect such reformation in the constitution of the House of Lords as would at least continue it in existence as a contributory branch of the legislature in the contingency which I have attempted to examine.

The next development historically which requires consideration is concerned with the position of the House of Lords. The constitutional powers of that body were, if asserted to the full compass of their theoretical scope, untenable and even mediæval. And yet wisely stewarded in a country so conservative they could have been made available for many generations. For the English political mind had no particular prejudice against the House of Lords or against the system, which so many Americans find it difficult to understand. If they had, the English monarchy could not have survived so long with a prestige which, as I shall show later, has not declined.

But the condition of the retention of the powers of the House of Lords was that those powers should not be too openly harnessed to the chariot of a particular party. The nation was not, indeed, on the whole unprepared that the exercise of its powers should be conservative in the non-political sense, but it was justly impatient of any attempt to make a constituent branch of the legislature a mere tool of a single party. And, therefore, a fatal mistake was made when that house compromised so many causes upon which the greatness of the country depended in the cause of that which was described in the cant of the moment as the People's budget.

All that was operative in that budget was and has since proved to be trash. It has been thrown since, with general approval, upon the political dust heap. But the House of Lords under bad advice, reasserting a prerogative, which unquestionably survived theoretically, but upon which no wise man should have insisted, brought itself into sharp and fatal collision with a powerful though fugitive wave of contemporary opinion.

No one can foresee the results. But this at least is certain, that until the House of Lords be reconstituted and re-formed Great Britain is the only country in the world which has at once an uncontrolled constitution and an ineffective second chamber. The House of Lords no doubt still retains a powerful instrument to insure delay. And this power may be very formidable. But it cannot be effective unless it is certain that the tenure of power of the government of to-day is fugitive, and in relation to all finance the House of Lords is powerless.

The extreme sections of the Conservative party never ceased to attack the coalition government because it did not reform the House of Lords. Mr. Asquith had affirmed and had broken his own solemn pledge to make this reform complete. The coalition government produced proposals which even if inadequate in relation to the ultimate problems would have mitigated the constitutional disabilities amid which we labour to-day.

The present Conservative government has done nothing, nor can I see any reason whatever for conjecturing that it can or will do anything. The critics of the British constitution are therefore entitled to point out, firstly, that we have a constitution at the mercy of a momentary gust of parliamentary opinion, and secondly, that we have no second chamber equipped with the political and constitutional power to resist such a gust. Looked at abstractedly, the position would appear to be hopeless. It would be hopeless to any one who has not studied the political and constitutional history of the English people.

But it is not the purpose of my address to-day to indicate the methods, if there be such, by which we may hope to disentangle ourselves from our present difficulty. It is, on the contrary, my purpose for the consideration of other constitutional lawyers to indicate the difficulties in which our recent political developments have involved the British constitution.

And now I pass to another topic. The British empire must on the whole be pronounced to be the most amazing congeries of self-governing communities which has ever spontaneously supported the fabric of a great empire. Ten years ago it was a fashionable subject of speculation among political writers whether that fabric could survive either the tests of peace or the tests of war. The tests of peace over a long period still remain to be probed.

Out of the crucible of war the British Empire has emerged on the whole as the most amazing phenomenon in history. And consistently with the whole development of British constitutional precedent nothing has been put in writing. All the premiers of all the dominions assisted in and made themselves responsible for the deliberations from which the Treaty of Versailles emerged. A new cabinet was formed. It was not the cabinet of the British Isles. It was the cabinet of the British Empire.

It was proposed by some one that the constitution of this new cabinet, a cabinet not unlikely to play a decisive part in the world's history for centuries, should be reduced to writing. Mr. Hughes, the Prime Minister of Australia, with equal flair and force disputed this view and carried his point. And so to-day it happens that the new constitution of the British Empire is attested by no record in any constitutional document.

But it is none the less true that there will never again be a formidable orientation of British policy, which has not obtained the assent of the Dominions. And it may, therefore, be moderately claimed that of all the changes which half a century has brought to English constitutional life, the most pregnant is that which has associated the great Dominions on equal terms with the British Foreign Office in everything which determines alike the domestic and international fortunes of the commonwealth.

I have no leisure to trace in detail the minor aspects of development, as many of them are, which the constitutional historians of the last fifty years must record. But this superficial survey would be incomplete in relation even to its own standards if it did not take some note of the changes, such as they may be, which fifty years have introduced in the position and prestige of the British monarchy.

Queen Victoria was a very masterful woman. With limitations she was even a great woman. But her conception of the monarchial prerogative would to-day have been impossible. Her bedchamber crisis, her dismissal of Lord Palmerston, and her nakedly avowed preference for Mr. Disraeli over Mr. Gladstone would in this age have been neither tolerable nor tolerated. But to make this admission is not to concede that the power of the monarchy has really declined.

On the contrary, the prestige of the monarchy and the influence of the monarchy in the prudent and conscientious hands of King George have rather waxed than waned. No great decision of state, it may confidently be claimed, is taken without close discussion with the sovereign. He cannot, and he would not, claim to deflect the clear view of a strong cabinet. But no cabinet, however strong, could afford to disregard the difficulties and doubts put forward by a sovereign who has no interest in party politics, and whose experience is reinforced by continuity and immutability.

The historian, therefore, who appraises the development of the British constitution must, on the whole, recognise that in a changing world the influence of the British monarchy has been preserved unchanged. The degree of the influence will no doubt vary with the personality of him or her who wears the crown. Queen Victoria had her special specialty and her special qualities. King Edward had his. King George, at the most difficult period of all, has accepted in his own person a kingly responsibility which has done as much to strengthen the British monarchy as any one of his predecessors since the constitution of England became a reality and not a theory.

The future of the world is incalculable. The decision is premature whether you, and those who agree with you, have been right in trying to control the free will of a free people by judicial authority, or whether we have been right in trusting the free will and a free people to work out their own salvation.

# CHAPTER VI

## CANADIAN BAR ASSOCIATION ADDRESS

### September 3, 1923

UNTIL the month of August, 1914, it was generally, though not quite completely, true that the civilised nations of the world had, over a long period of time, combined to increase the authority of international law. Indeed, from the days of Grotius there had, until ten years ago, been discernible a hardening tendency upon the "legal" side of a body of doctrine which never, of course, could, except metaphorically, be called law at all. The science of law has, throughout the ages, been the subject of much cultivated and learned controversy. But when the analysts like Austin had completed their analysis, and the historians like Maine had

168

completed their histories, there emerged
from their co-operative activities a general
recognition among writers upon jurisprudence that, whatever other quality is de-
manded by the conception of law, that of
compulsive assertion by a superior is vital
and indispensable. In other words, a law
is not a law unless some one superior to
yourself can penalise and chastise you for
its breach.

The earliest writers upon the subject of
international law were not only masters of
casuistry, not only consummate dialecti-
cians, they were also golden, incorrigible
optimists. For they found Europe as we
may even find it to-morrow—a welter of
savagery, a scene of desolation and abomina-
tion, amid which the garnered treasures of
Greek and Roman civilisation had perished.

To a man like Grotius, with a mind incredibly powerful and versatile, too shrewd
for self-illusion, it must have been plain how

slow, how painful, and how precarious must be the development of the tiny seedling which he planted with so much courage and so much hope. For many passages of his immortal work make it plain that he realised that it was not, and probably never would be, possible to assimilate international law with municipal law. And yet, with a bold and generous vision, he lavished all the powers of an incredibly well-endowed mind upon the attempt to fling an atmosphere of law around the moral code upon which, as he clearly saw, the whole fabric of future civilisation might, and almost certainly would, depend. Peering into the future, this remarkable man must almost certainly have reasoned to himself somewhat in this way:

*Moral Precepts.*

International law can never become a real law unless and until there is formed a concourse of nations able to agree upon that which shall be law; resolved to enforce it upon recalcitrant members; and armed, by mutual agreement, with the material force necessary to restrain and coerce those members of the international family who disobey its decrees. Such a League of Nations (I think Grotius may have said to himself) is little likely to arise in this imperfect world. But some progress is possible. The moral precepts which ought as surely to guide the actions of nations as those of individuals may be so camouflaged as law (though I hardly think he used the word) that in time the majority of civilised nations will tend more and more to accord to these moral precepts the actual authority of law. They will do so, I hope, because the majority in most countries will prefer to act morally rather than immorally. They will do so, at any rate, I believe, because most sensible statesmen will realise that on the whole it pays to behave decently and in the manner which most moral and educated men admit to be decent. The great fathers of international law would undoubtedly have expressed their meaning more formally, more lengthily, more eloquently, and perhaps I may be allowed to add, more pompously, but I am on certain ground, which I could justify by unlimited quotations, when I claim that their general outlook upon the nascent science to which they contributed so much genius and so much hope was of the kind which I have indicated. Optimists they undoubtedly were. All pioneers have been. No pioneers have ever brought more enthusiasm to a more tangled and more hopeless jungle.

Twenty-five years ago, I wrote a small work upon the subject of international law, in which I attempted a definition of that science. To-day it would be necessary that I should rewrite it. To-day I should define international law as that body of doctrine which civilised nations, until quite recently, had believed to be binding upon them with a force and authority comparable to that which in their own systems is conceded to their own law. This definition, of which I sorrowfully record my own conviction that it is neither cynical nor pessimistic, suggests some sombre observations. Hundreds of years have passed since the great pioneers addressed themselves to a Herculean task—hundreds of years of Christianity and civilisation—and yet to-day the cruel and poignant truth confronts him who cares to understand the truth that the Great War very nearly demonstrated the moral bankruptcy of that system which had been laboriously and painfully compiled by the humanitarian and intellectual effort of centuries.

The most familiar and elementary weakness of international law had, of course, always been that it formally recognised in war a permitted system of litigation. Implicit in this recognition was that the result of such a war, whatever its moral quality, possessed, even if by usurpation, the func-

173

tion of the judge. And accordingly, a nation which put its quarrel to the hazard of the sword established its legal—as apart from its moral—position by its successful employment.

This was the reason which led the cynical, unscrupulous, but powerful mind of Bismarck to pour constant contempt upon international law and its professors. "Find me an argument founded upon international law," he cried, "and I will find you a professor to answer it." And so the nation which worshipped in the world of abstract thought Treitschke, and in the world of action Bismarck, grew intelligibly contemptuous of a creed which perforce admitted that success constituted immorality. And so there arose in Europe a Power calculating, reckless, unscrupulous, which laughed at The Hague Conferences while it attended them; which looked only to the sharpness of its sword and to the disciplined strength of its great battalions.

# CANADIAN BAR ADDRESS

*The German Example.*

In the year 1914, all those who counted
intellectually and politically in Germany
were secretly laughing at international law
and all that it involved. And the tragic commentary cannot be omitted that the inherent
and unavoidable weakness of this body of
doctrine almost justified them in the view
which they took. For had Germany won
the War, what would have happened? She
would have dictated peace, I should imagine,
at Buckingham Palace; for the *réclame* of
this *mise en scène* would, on the whole, have
been greater than that of Versailles. And,
anyhow, she had enjoyed this once already.
She would have rewritten on a new map the
outlines of a new world. And all this she
would have done with complete impunity.
And, inasmuch as the strong have many
friends, she would have found apologists
and defenders in every neutral country of
the world. She would have conquered by the
agency of poison gas; by sinking hospital

ships; by breaking almost every hitherto observed convention of war; by converting the sea into a holocaust of murder; and by a public deification of the doctrine of dreadfulness. The triumph of Germany, in other words, would have involved the destruction and the disruption of international law as the whole world had understood that law until the month of August, 1914.

But Germany did not win the War. Through all those dark and doubtful months we had sustained ourselves by the belief that the defeat of Germany would mark the downfall of an outlook upon public law at once so unmoral and so destructive. Has it done so? Can any dispassionate observer, examining with cool survey the present outlook of the world, claim that the authority of international law is as strong to-day as it was in 1914? Central Europe is dissolving before our eyes into anarchy. It would exceed the purpose of this lecture to analyse and determine the responsibility. We are

more concerned to appraise facts than to
distribute praise or blame. And the facts,
however disillusioning, stare us in the face.
Every nation which, under the terms of the
Treaty of Peace, has obtained less than that
to which it conceived itself entitled, is simply
waiting an opportunity to get more. Nearly
every vital preclusion of the various Hague
conferences was violated in the Great War,
and no step has been taken, or can very
easily be taken, for restoring that which,
for want of a better term, I must describe
as their authority. The late Mr. Hall, in a
preface to the last edition but one of his
learned and sagacious work upon the subject of international law, indulged in a
gloomy prediction, which events have very
fully justified. He predicted that the next
war would be fought with a degree of unscrupulous savagery which had not been
known since the Middle Ages. He was right.

If we could persuade ourselves that the
defeat of Germany, the principal employer

of those methods, had ended them for ever, the mischief, in point of time, would be finite, and in point of consequence curable. But, unhappily, we have no such security. It is, on the whole, worth while to face facts, however disagreeable and naked those facts may be, and the truth is that when the nations of the world spring to arms, when the glittering counter of world dominion is placed at the hazard, all the boasted veneer of our civilisation is swiftly dissipated, and we still revert, as man reverted long ago, to the state of society which Mr. London so vividly portrayed in his book "Before Adam." Does any sane person now believe that, if another war should ever emerge, a nation which sees victory or defeat depending almost upon the throw of a coin will neglect any instrument of destruction, however devastating, the employment of which promises success and all that success brings? And indeed, I myself have always thought that the nice distinctions drawn by various

Hague Conferences between permissible and non-permissible instruments of destruction were so artificial that they could not support the harsh test of modern warfare.

## Submarines and Poison Gas.

Let me give an illustration, in order to see precisely where international law stands to-day. The unlimited submarine warfare carried on by Germany did as much to brand her with indelible infamy as any crime which she committed. Germany was defeated, and her fleet lies rotting in the green depths of Scapa Flow. With her defeat it might have been supposed that the judgment of the whole world had been finally and for all time delivered upon the method of warfare so inhumane and so murderous. Has it? Are we sure to-day that, if a world war broke out to-morrow in which this country was involved, the same submarine weapon would not be employed to our hurt? Is it not, on the contrary, a fact that every competent Admiralty in the world is at this moment preparing its plans upon the basis that the German menace will be renewed, if not by Germany, then by another? How are we, then, who up to the present have counted ourselves as writers and authorities on international law, to describe the legality of submarine warfare? Are we to say that it is legal or that it is illegal? And if we pronounce it to be illegal, are we, none the less, to proceed upon the basis that it will be recurrent, and that we must guard against it or perish?

A further illustration may be attempted. The last war ushered in the employment of poison gases. In comparison with the physical consequences of many gases, actual and potential, the nice refinements of The Hague Conferences become obsolete, and, if the subject were not too tragical, they would also become humorous. What are the chemists of the disappointed nations doing at this moment? Are they caring about The Hague

Conferences of the past or The Hague Conferences of the future? Is there any particular form of chemical horribleness from which Germany would recoil if she could destroy the French Army of Occupation on the Ruhr? Are we quite sure in the Temple of Truth from what weapons we should ourselves recoil if we were Germans and the French were in occupation, and perhaps not a merely temporary occupation, on the Ruhr? Have even the most skilful chemists finally exploited the destructive effects of new chemicals? Are new Hague Conferences to continue to proscribe expansive bullets and register preclusions upon the use of chemicals which hardly any nation in the world has any intention of obeying?

I am fully conscious that the whole tenor of my observations is one of gloomy presage to the future of civilisation, but my counsel, such as it is, has no value if it be not frankly and honestly given. There was, indeed, a dream, affording to sanguine minds the prospect of a golden hope, when President Wilson held out the assurance that the United States of America would adhere to a League of Nations which could have made international law a reality and armed its prescriptions with a sanction. I myself, unfortunately, have not a sanguine mind, or at least not an oversanguine one, and I never for one moment believed that President Wilson would be successful in inducing the American people to undertake responsibilities alien to its traditions, and only with great difficulty to be reconciled with its interests. And accordingly, I incurred no small degree of censure by directing attention, in an address which I delivered to the New York Bar Association, to the difficulties which, principally from the American point of view, seemed to me to make its adoption difficult, if not impossible. Unhappily, my premonitions were justified. I wish that my critics had been right and I had been wrong. But I knew then very

182

clearly that I was right and that they were wrong.

*The League of Nations.*

Who, for instance, with the claim to be still at large, could have supposed that the United States of America would have submitted to the League of Nations for imperative decision the question of Japanese immigration in her western provinces? It is a very noble thing to be an idealist; but it is, on the whole, more useful to be a realist. If the League of Nations had been practicable in the sense that the United States of America would have done everything necessary to make it a success—in the sense, to be more precise, that the United States of America would have contributed her share of the military and naval force necessary to enforce its decisions—a fair opportunity would at least have been given to a dazzling experiment. Then, and then only, might international law have become law in the only sense in which any law is law. But even so, I hesitate, while I would have welcomed the experiment, to predict with complete conviction that it would have succeeded. Would immunity, even so, have been attainable in any grave decision which required instruments of coercion? And, in a supreme clash of nations and of interests, would anything else have happened except that a new world war would have developed with alignments more clearly defined?

My conclusions, therefore, though sombre, are, I believe, sensible and cautious. Mankind is a combative animal. The world still holds precious and incalculable prizes for those who have the will to conquer and the manhood to die. Nations will still be found willing to put all to the hazard; men will still be found in those nations willing to die. And so the survival of the fit and the elimination of the unfit will still proceed, and all that we, who call ourselves international lawyers, can hope to do is to carry in hands less puissant the torch of Grotius, and preach to an indifferent world the creed that in the long run violence and illegality do not pay; that, to a nation, the white escutcheon of unsullied morality is as priceless as to an individual, and that the Sermon on the Mount was not the idle chatter of a thought-less Man.

# CHAPTER VII

## IDEALISM IN INTERNATIONAL POLITICS

IDEALISM may be defined, as well as in another way, by calling it the spirit which impels an individual or group of individuals to a loftier standard of conduct than that which ordinarily prevails around him or them. This definition does not, of course, impinge upon the philosophical concept of idealism that in external conceptions the objects immediately known are ideas; that, in other words, all reality is in its nature psychical. With such abstractions (though they are of great interest) we are not practically at this moment concerned.

Idealism in the international field is the spirit which would carry into the relations of States the kind of ethical progress generally indicated above.

Now it is evident that every sane and normal citizen must desire improvement in the standards of purity and morality. Nor is it less evident that every reasonable statesman must desire that the relationship between States shall be increasingly regulated in accordance with the highest attainable standards of conscientious conduct. Conflict, therefore, is very unlikely to arise so long as attention is confined to the larger generalisations which the term suggests. The subject, however, of this observation is naturally neither an attempt to examine nor appraise the value either in national or international affairs of a loftier standpoint or of a more austere ethical outlook. Such abstract discussion would be one-sided; nor would it lend itself to any fruitful disputation.

It is when attention is directed to the sharply contrasted views of those who are distinguished in political matters as "Idealists" or "Realists" that the subject matter

187

of the present examination becomes apparent. The use of these discordant terms makes it plain that the word "Idealism" is employed in current phraseology to indicate a point of view in relation to life which may be challenged without either absurdity or cynicism. No one, for instance, imagines that the school of political thought which is conveniently described as Realistic would impeach the conception or definition of Idealism with which this address began. The term, therefore, is used in a narrower or more specialised sense, which must be somewhat more carefully analysed. In current language an idealist in this sense is one who places before himself in private or public affairs as attainable a goal which other citizens, perhaps equally moral, do not believe to be so attainable. Provided that the idealist be a sound judge of moral valuations, nothing but good can proceed from his admonitions. If he wrenches in his individual exertions even a tiny fragment from the area of a grosser world he will not perish without the glory of achievement. It has, of course, naturally happened that the greatest of idealists have been teachers or preachers. And of all such Jesus Christ was evidently the most pre-eminent. But it would be unreasonable to suppose that when He admonished him who was assaulted to turn the other cheek to the smiter, or him who was rich to sell all his possessions and give them to the poor, He was laying down standards of conduct which He either expected or desired to see generally adopted. He was, on the contrary, diffusing through the medium of metaphor a sweet and beautiful moral atmosphere for the purification of imperfect manhood. Were an autocrat to issue a ukase within his own dominions ordering all rich men to divest themselves of their possessions in favour of the poor, he would be, assuming morality of purpose, an idealist in the narrower sense, but he would also be an idealist in that more ag-

189

gressive and dangerous connotation, with which we are principally concerned. An analysis of the subject derives some guidance from the use of the term in private as opposed to public policy. For such an examination makes it plain how small has been the conquest of Idealist thought, even over the comparatively easy domain of individual conduct. The school of Idealism is the very antithesis of the school of self-interest. And yet nothing is more apparent than that politically, economically, and philosophically, the motive of self-interest not only is, but must be and ought to be the mainspring of human conduct. Bentham long since pointed out in his "Theory of Legislation" how inconvenient and even mischievous the consequences would be if every individual were to regulate his conduct, not in relation to his own interests, which he is likely to understand, but in relation to the interests of others, in relation to which he is very likely to be imperfectly informed. Economically the matter is not less plain. Mankind subsists precariously upon this globe on the terms of constant and contributory toil. The experience of thousands, perhaps of hundreds of thousands of years, has shown that the desire of self-advancement is the only adequate incentive for that standard of labour and achievement which each individual must be encouraged in the common scheme to afford. The only legitimate sphere, therefore, of the idealist within the field of private morality is to elevate, if he can, the standards by reference to which conduct is, in the existing scheme of things, adjusted, without attempting to impair motives which are fundamental in human nature and vital to social economy.

If we turn to the relationship of States we shall find it necessary to draw similar distinctions even more clearly; for many causes combine in this field to contract the area with which altruism is likely to win adherence. The man who cries, "My country, right or wrong," may or may not be a patriot; but he is certainly not an idealist. The latter in this connection must again be conceived of not merely as one who desires to see the substitution in international practice of Law for War: the complete purification of international morality; and perhaps "The Parliament of Man, the Federation of the World." For in this vague sentiment of benevolence many admirable citizens of many countries would concur. But the idealist in the sense which concerns us is he who believes that these things are in fact attainable; that we ought to take steps and make exertions, and even sacrifices, in order to attain them. And he would indeed, in most cases, actually shape the policy of his country, and even compromise its interests, because he believes in the prospects which he indicates and in the sanctity and infallibility of international compacts.

# INTERNATIONAL POLITICS

Twenty-four years ago a Czar of Russia issued to the world a very sonorous and idealist message. It announced the hope that war might be for ever ended. It made specific proposals in that sense. And thus there came into existence a Hague Conference, with the history of which most of us are familiar. It would be foolish to deny that this Conference did some useful work in its secondary tasks—namely, the consideration of international disputes and the alleviation of avoidable cruelty in the prosecution of war, which is itself in its very essence cruel. But it has achieved absolutely nothing in the direction of its major and more imposing purpose. In a book upon the subject of international law which I wrote immediately after the appearance of the Czar's communication I made the following observation:

"No sensible person with the slightest knowledge of history will believe that human nature has so profoundly altered as to afford the most remote prospect that this dream will ever be realised."

This conclusion was much assailed at the time by our sentimentalists. But a few years later that same Russia was hurling men in millions in the attempt to destroy Japan. And continuously thereafter the junta of evil and ambitous men, of whom the Kaiser was alike the mouthpiece and the figurehead, was projecting the stupendous tragedy which has almost, in its reactions, destroyed the civilisation of Europe. Untaught by previous experience, undeterred by the shattering refutation of their beliefs which the Great War brought with it, the idealists immediately had the originality to exploit its outbreak for their own controversial purposes. It was indeed unfortunate, they admitted, that the War should have occurred at all, and especially war so savagely conducted and flung over so enormous an area of the world's surface. But, after all, it had its bright side. For it was to be "a war to end war." This time, at least, when once the ploughshare, according to the correct tradition, had ousted the weapons of war, there was to be no further declension into primeval savagery. And so we were to have a League of Nations consisting in time of all the nations, great and small, in the world, equipped with military and naval force, and therefore able to make good its decisions against a recalcitrant member.

While I thought and think that there was and still is a modest area within which the League of Nations may make useful contribution to the harmony of the world, the larger claims made on its behalf always seemed to me to be frankly fantastic. Its framers forgot human nature as absurdly as they neglected history. What in the history of the world has ever happened which afforded foothold for expectations so megalomaniac? Divide the history of the world into two broad epochs, with the birth of

Jesus Christ as the dividing line. An examination in terms however general of these two periods equips a scientific observer with some material for the formation of true decision. Of the earlier period first.

I do not pause to deal here with the countless minor struggles which everywhere marked the infancy of the world. I mention, only to note it, the evidence collected by Darwin and his followers, showing at work in every department of life the survival of the fittest. But I must bestow a moment upon the lessons to be derived from the Old Testament. According to Holy Writ the chosen people were set in motion in order that they might violently possess themselves of a land flowing with milk and honey. They are "utterly to destroy their enemies." And thereafter we find them over a long period of time, protracted no doubt by their own peccadillos, engaged in violent and bloody strife with various antagonists. It may, of course, be said, in view of their desperate struggles with the Philistines, that the latter were very wicked men. Unfortunately, however, there always have existed in the world wicked men. Perhaps, therefore, it is necessary to import the qualification that all wars are to cease, except against very wicked men. But even here a difficulty presents itself. For every war that I know of has recurrently presented the same phenomenon that each protagonist believed, or pretended to believe, in the moral vileness of the other. In 1914, for instance, the French affirmed the Germans to be wicked aggressors, whereas the German people as a whole loudly proclaimed the criminal initiative of Russia. It must, therefore, I think, be admitted that the history of the chosen people, and indeed the Old Testament, taken as a whole, afford little ground for optimism in this regard. A similar but more extended observation fails to be made about all the great Eastern Empires of the ancient world. Indeed, in this connection sombre images throng the mind. Egyptians, Medes, Persians, Assyrians—all these achieved empire at the point of the sword. Of how many dead empires does the silent and immoble East contain the record? In what graves repose the millions of their unprotesting slain?

A happier and more humane experience might have been looked for from that exquisite intellectual efflorescence which we associate with the greatest of Greek States. Yet historically their records tell of almost continuous strife. So bitterly indeed, and amid such jealousies, did they wage war with one another that they could not combine even against the fierce Macedonian, and so one more rare and beautiful civilisation perished utterly from the earth.

To Greece succeeded Rome, teaching the entire world through the whole of its stern, dominating, and Imperial sway, that might was right, and that a sharp sword in the hand of a disciplined soldier was the most persuasive argument in world diplomacy.

And there came, too, in correction, the message of Jesus Christ, tender in its simplicity, superhuman in its humanity. The creed of Him who was crucified was to spread with incredible swiftness over a large part of the world's surface. Mighty powers and great princes have rendered homage to the message of mercy and peace which came from those divine and persuasive lips. And yet, while we take note of the spread of the Christian religion, we must none the less ask what has been its reaction upon international conduct? What was its influence over the recent world convulsion? What was its spiritual and intellectual contribution to that poignant problem? Why did an omnipotent Deity suddenly doom so many innocent victims to bestial destruction? Did the greatest priest in the world, enthroned in his Roman palace, ever pronounce a clear and intelligible conclusion upon the moral responsibility for the outbreak of war or upon the methods by which that war was conducted? Was he influenced by the fact that his flock diverged beneath different standards? If so, he ceased to be the divinely appointed mouthpiece of the higher morality and declined to a place, such as it was, among the politicians.

After a digression, apparently, rather than actually, irrelevant, we may resume a hurried historical summary.

After Rome, the Barbarians; after the Barbarians countless decades of anarchical chaos. And then throughout the centuries a long succession of almost uninterrupted wars—wars dynastic; wars territorial; wars on points of honour; and wars of naked aggression. England and France; England and Spain; England and Holland; England and France again; France and Germany; and thereafter the violent emergence of the Hohenzollern dynasty, more cynically based on blood and iron, more determined *debel-*

*lare superbos* than any Power since mighty Rome.

Are we really to learn nothing from all that has happened over this immense period of time? Does any warrant exist for the belief that human nature has altered its whole character? And, if so, what is the warrant? And when did that alteration take place? And, more particularly, what evidence of this great reformation do we find in what has happened in Europe since the Armistice? There have been wars and rumours of wars. I do not myself know of a moment in the last four years in which there has appeared to be less prospect of permanent peace in Europe than at the present moment. Nor is it an answer to say, as some do, that the infirmities of the Treaty of Versailles were responsible for the unrest and the violence which distract Europe to-day. If there were infirmities in that Treaty these again were infirmities in human nature which cannot be corrected. For the statesmen who put their names to that Treaty—to the territorial readjustments of that Treaty—were themselves the mouth-pieces of imperious and conquering democracies, and the views under discussion here are largely founded upon the expectation that the human nature of democracies will not undergo much modification. And if it does not they will obtain statesmen malleable to their purposes.

Summing up this branch of the matter, we are bound to conclude that from the very dawn of the world man has been a combative animal. To begin with, he fought violently for his own elemental needs; later, perhaps in tribal or communal quarrel; later still, with the growth of greater communities, upon a larger and more sophisticated scale. And it is to be specially noted that there have nevertheless almost always existed men who sincerely but very foolishly believed, firstly, that no war would arise in their own day; and, secondly (when that war did arise), that for some reason or other it would be the last. At this point the idealist degenerates into the pacifist; and it is at this point consequently that he becomes a danger to the community of which he is a citizen. Athens, in her decline, had no lack of such advisers; and, unhappily for the City of the Violet Crown, she preferred their sloppy folly to the ardent eloquence of Demosthenes. In the days of Napoleon (who had a very just contempt for these "idealogues") Charles Fox harnessed his eloquence to the chariot of sentimentalism. But he switched rather abruptly as soon as he became Prime Minister. And in our own day we have been afforded convincing evidence of the real peril to national security which arises when idealists grow too strong in the conduct of public affairs. Perhaps this happened in 1906. Every sensible person now realises that even in that year the German scheme was being nebulously conceived; and its deadly menace increased with every year which passed. I myself in a book called "Unionist Policy," published in 1910, devoted a long article, of which I shall presume to say that it was closely and clearly reasoned, to demonstrating the soundness of Lord Roberts' warnings. But the immense increase in the German Army, the construction of strategic railways upon the Belgian boundary, the creation of a mighty fleet, left our idealists unconvinced.

And accordingly every year the annual meeting of a great federation, with pathetic faith and sincerity, passed resolutions in favour of reducing our military and naval expenditure; and a member of Parliament, in private life an admirable citizen and a sagacious chemist, produced the immortal saying that he would rather trust to the doctrines of international law than to the protection of the British Fleet. Even the robust patriotism of my dear friend Mr. Winston Churchill succumbed for a fugitive moment to the miasma, though the lapse in his case was to be nobly retrieved by the demoniac energy elicited by actual contact with the Admiralty. It was, indeed, in these years that Idealism became rampant with those in power. Notorious and almost vital facts were everywhere ignored. German editors were entertained by English editors in London, and dilated with fluent eloquence upon the pacific intentions of the Fatherland. English editors in their turn visited Berlin to enjoy, in that martial capital, the same agreeable reassurances.

And all the time the armies grew. All the time a mighty instrument was being fashioned in the German fleet. All the time Heligoland frowned more impregnably upon the North Sea. All the time those great military railways, unneeded for peaceful traffic, were debouching upon the defenceless Belgian frontier. In the welter of sentimentality, amid which Great Britain might easily have mouldered into ruin, my valued colleague, Lord Haldane, presented a figure alike interesting, individual, and arresting. In speech fluent and even infinite, he yielded to no living idealist in the easy coinage of sentimental phraseology. Here, indeed, he was a match for those who distributed the chloroform of Berlin. Do we not remember, for instance, that Germany was his spiritual home? But he none the less prepared himself, and the Empire, to talk when the time came with his spiritual friends in language not in the least spiritual. He devised the Territorial Army, which was capable of becoming the easy nucleus of national conscription, and which unquestionably ought to have been used for that purpose at the outbreak of war. He created the Imperial General Staff. He founded the Officers' Training Corps.

And two other names require special and honourable mention in an age of incredible self-deceit. Lord Roberts devoted the evening of an illustrious life to warnings of marvellous prescience which passed almost unheeded. General Baden-Powell used the laurels which he had gained at Mafeking to inspire and sustain the noblest and most promising movement which has taken place in our lifetime. The foundation of the Boy Scouts established for this gifted and imaginative soldier a monument more lasting than bronze.

It has been thought worth while to retrace the events of these fateful years with some particularity in order to show that Idealism in national affairs is not merely impracticable, but that it may easily degenerate into a deadly source of national peril.

Still a further illustration may be drawn from recent events. The signing of the Armistice immediately released all the sentimentalists. Not only was the Great War ended, but there was never to be another. The League of Nations was to be equipped with functions and resources which would in effect enthrone it in super-sovereignty over the contributory nations. But herein the statesman who of all others should most completely have understood the American people demonstrated that in fact he understood them least of all. That people is the most generous people in the world in the field of international charity. The United States have lavished countless millions of dollars upon the starving population of Russia. They were first in the field with bountiful relief to stricken Japan. But they draw—and rightly draw—a sharp and logical distinction between Idealism in their capacity as private citizens for private charities and Idealism in their corporate or national character. And accordingly they exercised their undoubted right in repudiating at the first opportunity an idealist conception which they believed to be at once impracticable, strange to their traditions, and incompatible with their national interests.

A broader consideration must now in its turn be examined. We are told that the object aimed at is the abolition of war. Everybody recognises that war is both cruel and hateful. But is it even conceivable that it can ever be abolished? Is the ownership of the world to be stereotyped by perpetual tenure in the hands of those who possess its different territories to-day? If it is, very strange and undesirable consequences will one day follow. For nations wax and wane, so that a Power competent in one age to govern an empire, perhaps remote, in the general interest of the world, will in another abuse a dominion for which it no longer possesses the necessary degree of vigour. The history of Spain supplies a familiar illustration.

Her chivalry was second to none in Europe. Her high standard of gallant conduct was disfigured only by the cruelties of the Inquisition. Her stately galleons brought a quiver of apprehension even to the stout bosom of Queen Elizabeth and were never discredited until the rout of her superb Armada. And in exuberant colonial enterprise she was the mistress and pioneer of Europe. In the last-named enterprise, indeed, she flung her civilisation and her language into the remote parts of the world, deriving incredible titles from successive Papal Bulls. And coincidently or almost so with her immense maritime enterprise she flung the martial Moor in rout from Spain. But her decline was as rapid as her ascension. She proved no adequate custodian for her oversea possessions. Had a League of Nations existed when she began to lose them, would it have sustained Spain or the insurgents of Spain, or in another case, the despoilers of Spain?

And the general extrusion of savage races from regions—for instance, the American continent and certain of the South Sea Islands—to which they had some considerable legal right, shows that, rightly or wrongly, nations of stronger fibre, confronted by indigenous weaklings, have always asserted the right of forcible expropriation. No one (to make the argument short) who has studied the history of the world has ever defended the view that the supreme interest of evolutionary humanity can support a definitive delimitation for all time of the surface of the world.

But if such a final distribution is impracticable and even undesirable, by what agency are modifications to be made? Voluntary cessions of territory have not been frequent in the past; and there seems little reason to suppose that they will become more fashionable in the future. For many thousands of years the emergence of new and martial nations has been gradually marked by violent readjustments of national boundaries. It may, of course, be the case that human nature has so completely altered that some new method is discoverable. I confess, however, that none has up to the present occurred to my own mind.

It may, perhaps, be charged against those

who sincerely hold the views which I have attempted to make plain, that we carry in our veins the virus which coloured the sombre and unmoral genius of Treitschke, and which found popular expression in the mosquito propaganda of Von Bernhardi. But such a charge, if made, would be patently unjust. We neither hold nor have we preached these doctrines. We diagnose certain diseases. We did not create them. A distinction must surely be drawn between him who calls attention to the risk of conflagration and that other who puts his torch to inflammable material.

The purpose and moral of these general observations may be summarised in a few concluding observations. For as long a time as the records of history have been preserved human societies passed through a ceaseless process of evolution and adjustment. This process has been sometimes pacific, but more often it has resulted from warlike disturbance. The strength of different nations, measured in terms of arms, varies from century to century. The world continues to offer glittering prizes to those who have stout hearts and sharp swords; it is therefore extremely improbable that the experience of future ages will differ in any material respect from that which has happened since the twilight of the human race. It is for us, therefore, who in our history have proved ourselves a martial rather than a military people, to abstain, as has been our habit, from provocation; but to maintain in our own hand the adequate means for our own protection, and, so equipped, to march with heads erect and bright eyes along the road to our Imperial destiny.

THE END